My Italian Story

MY ITALIAN STORY

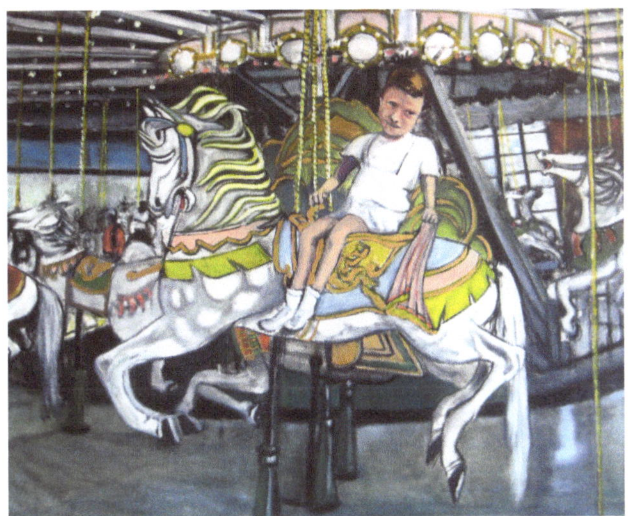

My Boyhood in Park Slope, Brooklyn 1941–1970s

Stories and Original Paintings

by Pacifico A. Palumbo

Pacifico A. Palumbo
info@greenemporium.com

Printed in the United States.

ISBN 978-1-7327843-2-1

Booksmyth Press
Shelburne Falls, MA
www.booksmythpress.com

*To my family and friends,
with a special thanks to my
publisher, Maureen Moore, and my
friend and editor, John McMillian.
Without their help this book would
not have been possible.*

INTRODUCTION

I can't remember a time when I wasn't doing something artistic or creative. I got my first set of oil paints when I was three years old. My Uncle Freddie, a lover of jazz and all things artistic, must have seen some potential in me because one day he showed up at my parents' house with some brushes and paints he'd bought as gifts for me from Macy's. I've rarely been away from the canvas ever since.

The only time I put down my brushes was when I was 27 years old and just beginning what would be a successful career as an advertising art director. I worked with Mary Wells in the 1960s and was fortunate to also work with Milton Glaser on creating the now iconic I Love New York campaign. Those years spent dreaming up ad campaigns were lots of fun—I consider myself to be one of the original "Mad Men"—but eventually I grew tired of the business, the corporate grind, the daily deadlines, so I quit and returned to my first love: art.

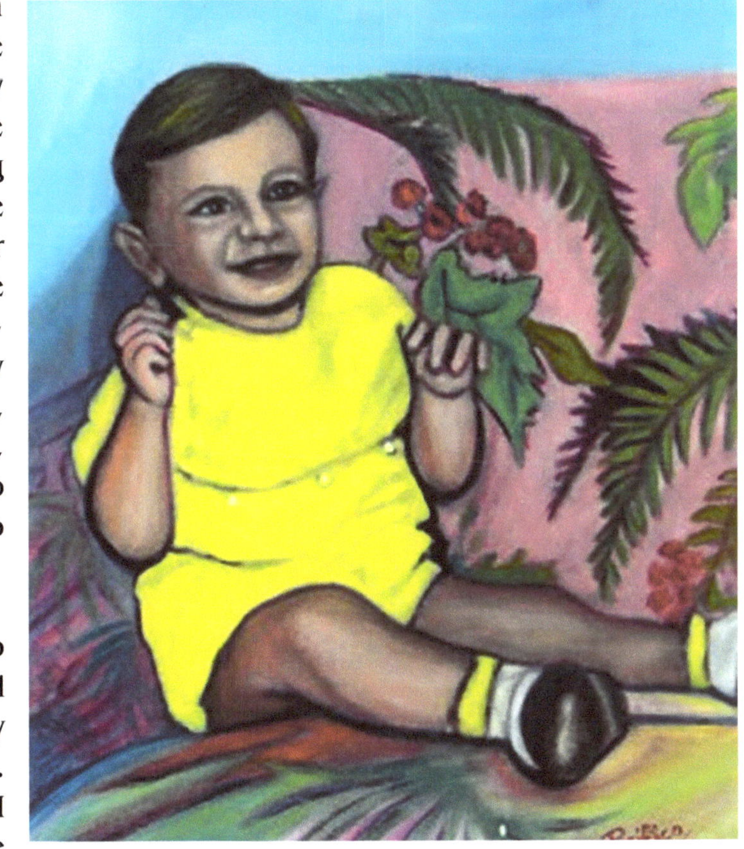

In 1977, I moved to Greenwich Village and opened a neon gallery called Say It In Neon. Through the years, I have become quite well known for my neon sculptures and installations; however, what I've always wanted to do is create an exhibition of oil paintings that tell the story of my life as an Italian growing up in Park Slope in Brooklyn, New York, in the 1940s and 1950s. Mine was a colorful childhood filled with colorful characters.

The paintings you see in this book reflect the experiences and people—aunts, uncles, cousins, friends—who shaped my life and created such a vibrant, rich and close-knit community in which to grow up.

The inspiration for this series came from a collection of black-and-white and color photographs that I had accumulated over the years. I'm lucky: my family loved taking pictures. At every occasion—even funerals—someone had a camera. I have boxes and boxes full of photographs, and each image sparks a memory or a story that, in turn, has inspired a painting.

One of the earliest memories I have is of going to visit my maternal grandmother. She was born here in America, but her parents arrived in the U.S. from Italy. When I visited, I was always drawn to a photograph in her parlor. The photo was ripped, and she'd never tell me why. Later, I found out that my grandfather died when he was 33 years old, leaving my grandmother on her own with five young children to take care of. She was so distraught and so in love with my grandfather that she just wanted to die, so she ripped herself out of the photo. My mother, who was only 10 when her father died, ended up raising her younger sisters and brother while my grandmother spent most of her days in a rocking chair, mourning the death of her husband.

There are other stories, too. After my father's father died, the family took a photograph. Back then, it was customary to take a picture of the remaining family members. My paternal grandmother had 11 children: six girls and five boys. Every boy she had before my father came along died. She named my father Anthony and prayed to St. Anthony every day to keep him alive. She would bring her young son to the church, where he later became an altar boy, and would dress him as a monk on the Feast of St. Anthony. For years, you could always find my grandmother praying the rosary to thank St. Anthony for keeping her own Anthony alive. They called my grandmother a saint. My father, Anthony, died in 1991 at the age of 79.

One of my favorite subjects was my Aunt Helen. She was so much fun. She came to live with us after her husband, Joe, died so that my father could afford the brownstone of his dreams (in 1955, it cost $12,500). Aunt Helen had her own apartment on the third floor, but she'd spend most of her time with us.

She was such a hoot, and joker that she was, it was only appropriate that her birthday was April 1. When she turned 50, we threw a big party for her and at one point I told her that I wanted to take her picture. Always up for anything, she said, "Let's have some fun." She went into her closet and after a few minutes came out wearing a velvet green bridesmaid's dress. Where she got it from, who knew? Then she took all the bows from her birthday presents and put them in her hair. Just as I was about to take her picture, she yelped, "Wait!" She needed one more prop. She spotted the colorful plastic flowers on the coffee table next to her, grabbed them and placed them in her lap.

Perfect, she said. I snapped the photo.

Years later, I wanted to paint a portrait of her. It took me a while to get started. I remember staring at the blank canvas, willing my Aunt Helen to come to life again so that I could capture her true essence, to show her as she truly was. She was funny and kind and loving, and I wanted all of that to come through in the portrait. As I painted, I began to cry, remembering the day I'd snapped the photo of her in her green dress. This lasted for more than a half hour, which is how long it took me to paint Aunt Helen. You can see the finished portrait in this book.

Let me tell you one more story. It's a good one. One Sunday afternoon, after returning home from the Army with a new Nikon F camera in hand, I visited my parents' house. My mother, dressed in a colorful muumuu, was in the kitchen, making her famous lasagna for traditional Sunday dinner. Her sauce was bubbling in a big pot on the Maytag stove and she was sitting at the Formica table, unraveling the lasagna into a baking dish. I said, "Ma, look at me." She turned and smiled as I took her picture.

After photographing that moment, I went outside to the garden, where I saw my Uncle Phillie talking to our neighbor Jennie. He was leaning against the fence, looking macho and confident. Jennie, her hair in curlers, had a wide smile on her face. She was clearly enraptured by what he was saying. Her elbows were hanging over the gate, which was open slightly, and if she slipped or pushed any harder she would have stumbled into my family's garden. At the time, I didn't much think of what they could have been talking about. What I noticed, instead, was the perfect light that surrounded them, and the beauty of the garden, with its grape vines and roses. Without them knowing, I snapped a quick photo and kept on walking.

About five years ago, I showed that picture to my uncle's daughter Susan. As soon as I handed the photo to her, she gasped. "That's her! That's her!" she cried. "That's the SOB that my father cheated on my mother with."

Later, I re-created that garden scene in a painting I called *"Gumada"* from the southern Italian slang for "mistress.".

I'll save the rest of my stories for the paintings on the pages inside. I hope that by reading about my life and encountering my artwork you'll think of your own family and where you came from.

Everyone has a story to tell.

I hope you enjoy my Italian story.

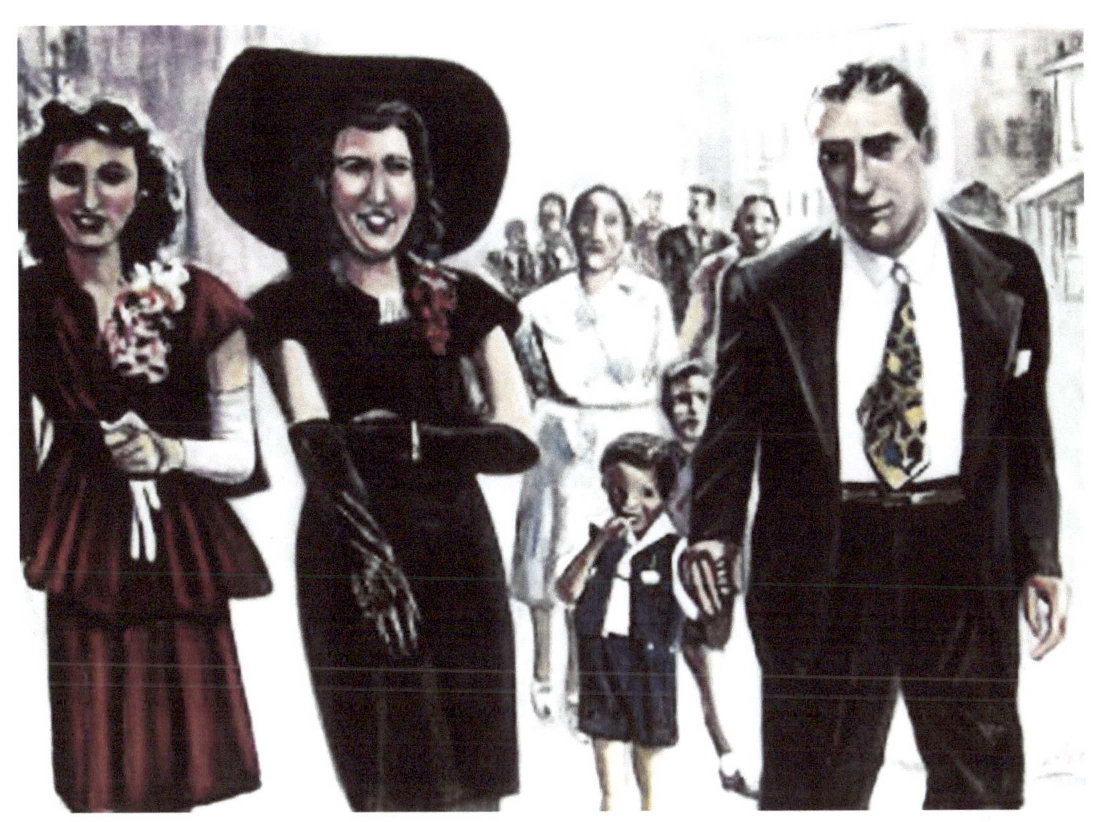

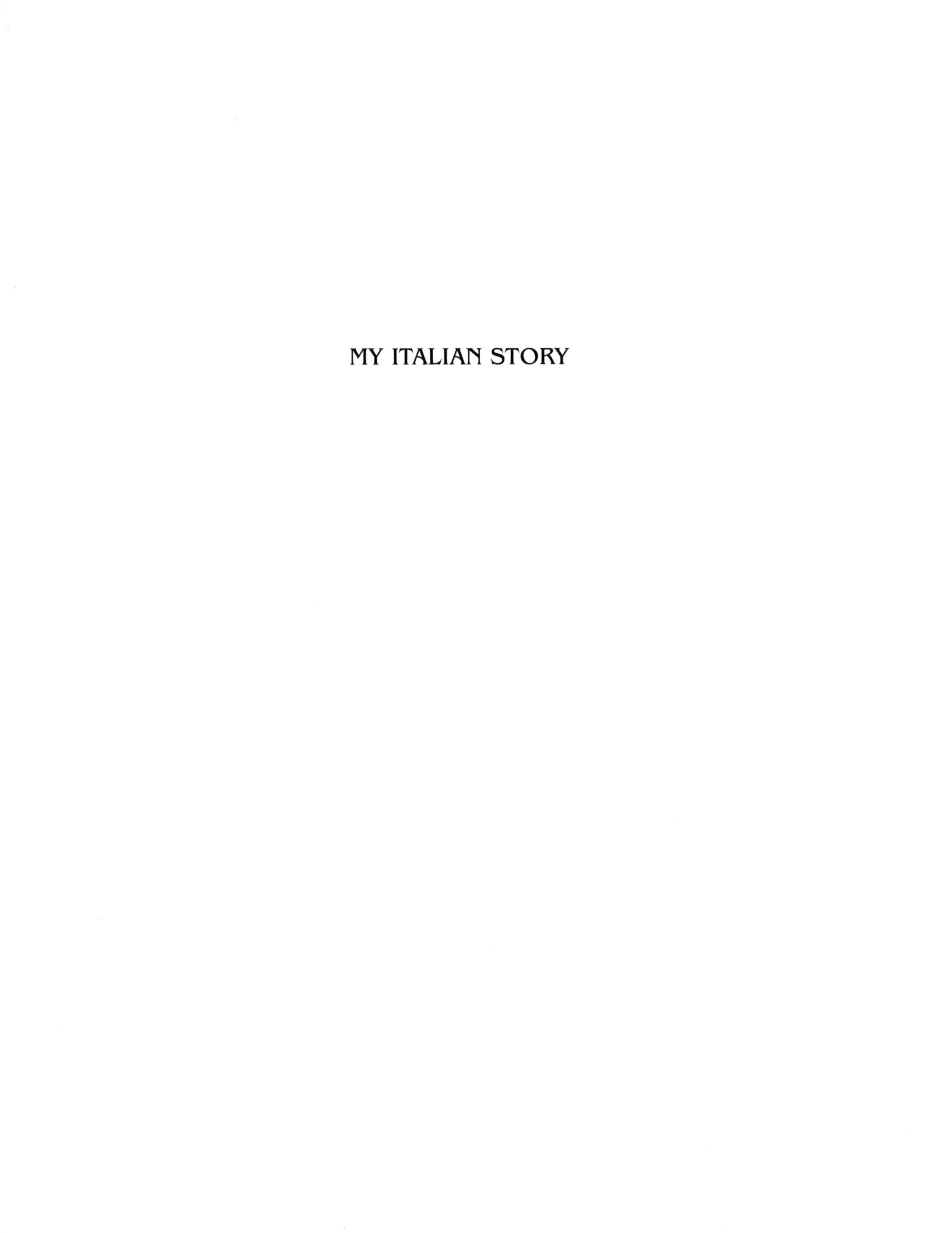

MY ITALIAN STORY

ME, THE BABY

I was born on April 4, 1941, in Park Slope, Brooklyn. This is a painting of me sitting, smiling happily, on my parents' colorful couch. I loved all the colors of it. That's probably why I was a very happy baby.

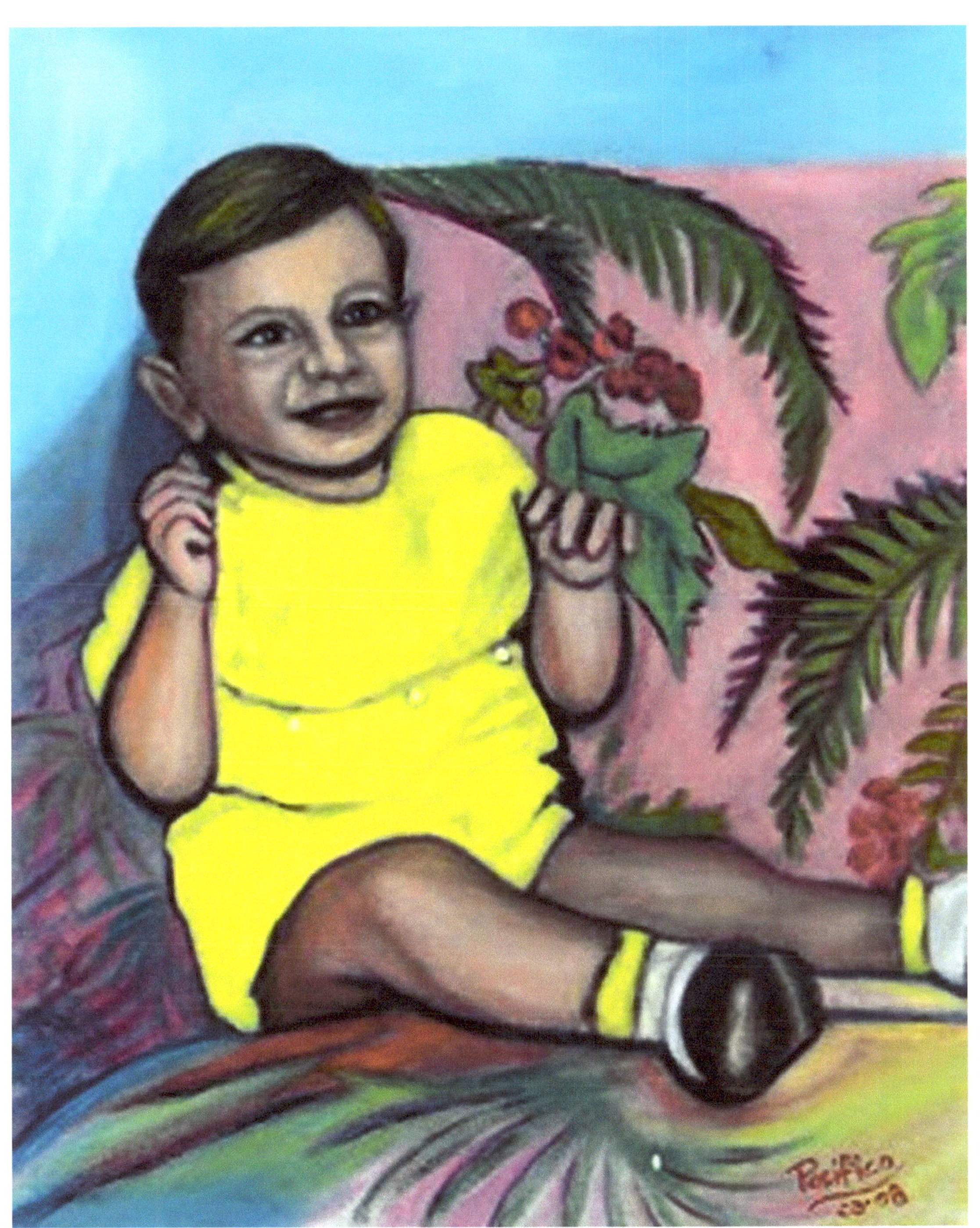

DADDY'S LITTLE GIRL

One of my earliest memories is of visiting my maternal grandmother. She was born here in America, but her parents arrived in the U.S. from Calabria and Naples.

At her home, I was always drawn to a photograph she had placed on the fireplace mantel in her parlor. She had ripped herself out of the picture, and whenever I asked her why she refused to explain what happened. Later, I found out that she fell into a deep state of mourning following the death of my grandfather at the age of 33. My grandmother was so in love with him that she just wanted to die after he was gone, so she eliminated any evidence of her own existence in the photo. He left her alone with five young children to take care of. My mother, who was only 10 when her father died, ended up raising her younger sisters and brother while my grandmother spent most of her days in a rocking chair, mourning the death of her husband.

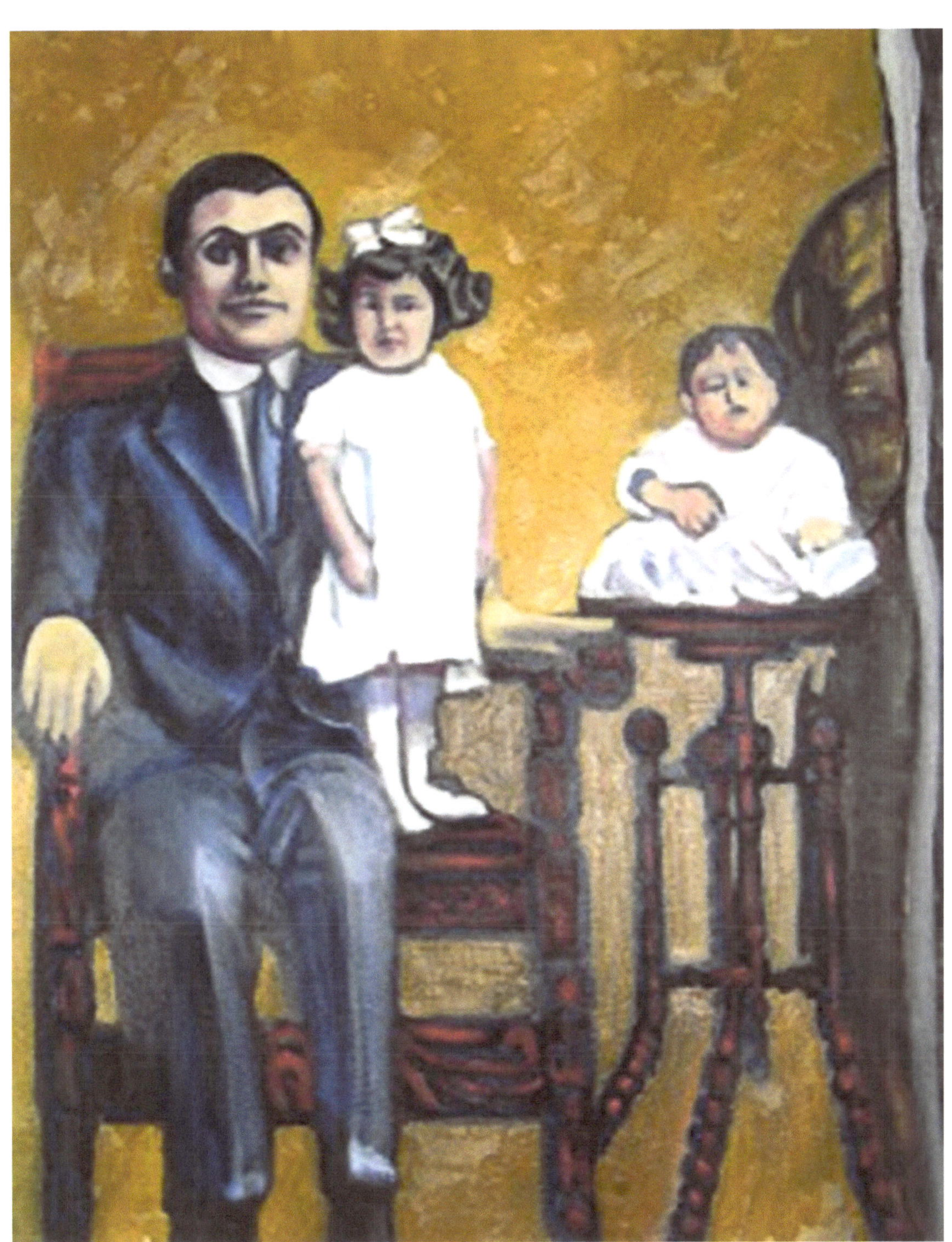

FATHER AS ALTAR BOY

This is my father. His name is Anthony. This painting is based on a studio portrait of him as an altar boy. He looks very angelic dressed in his cassock. I added *The Ecstasy of St. Anthony* behind him.

To my grandmother, my father was indeed a miracle baby. She had 11 children. Before my father arrived, she had lost all five of her boys. When my father was born, my grandmother spent her days praying to St. Anthony to let him live. Every year on June 13, the Feast St. Anthony, she would dress my father as a monk and take him to the church to join in the procession of St. Anthony.

He lived to be 79.

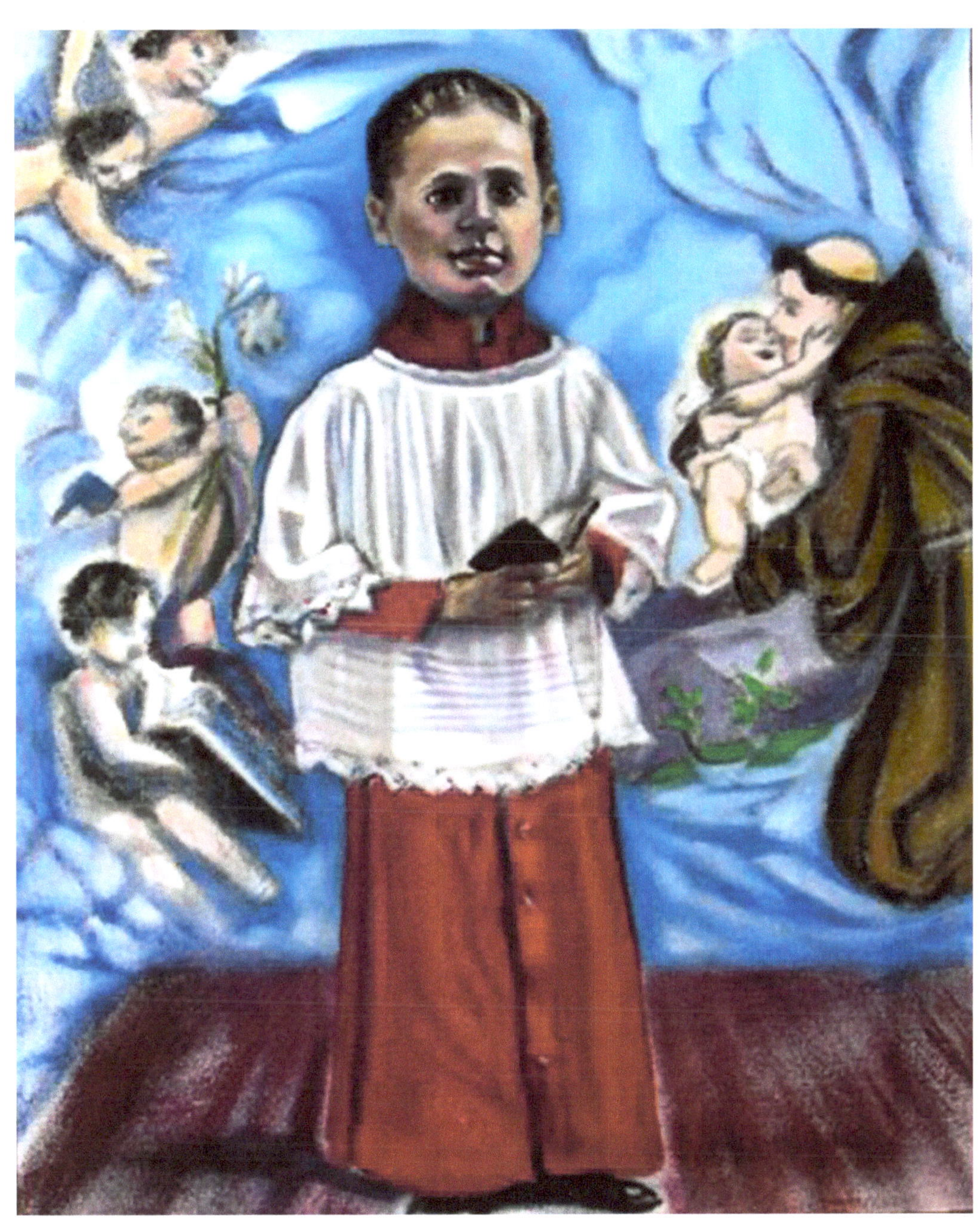

THE GATES OF HEAVEN

This is a painting of my father with his mother and his sisters. It was customary back then to take a photograph after the passing of an important person in a family. This time it was my grandfather. We see my grandmother surrounded by her daughters and my father. She had 11 children, six girls and five boys.

From left to right are Rosie; Julia; Beatrice; my father, Anthony; my grandmother, Mary Anthony or Marie Anthone, as my mother would say; Anna to her right; and in front of her, Louisa, her youngest. Madeline, my grandmother's oldest, is not in the picture.

They called my grandmother a saint, so I thought adding a background depicting the gates of heaven was particularly appropriate.

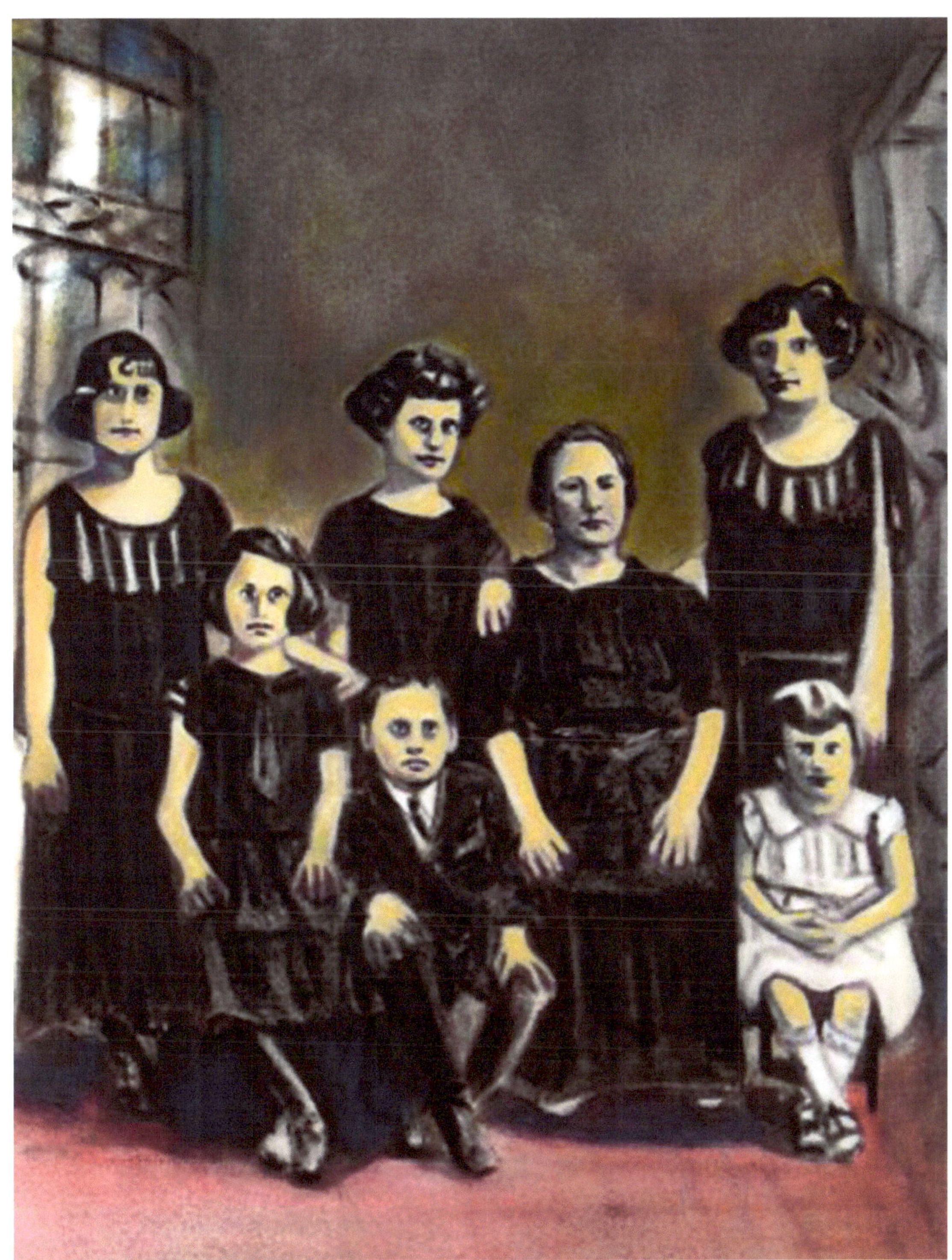

GRANDMOTHER

My grandmother was a very strong lady. The photo upon which this painting is based was taken at a cousin's wedding. I said, "Grandma, I want to take your picture." She put her hand on my cousin's and gave me a big smile. Through all her troubles she always managed to keep her composure.

She lived to be 87.

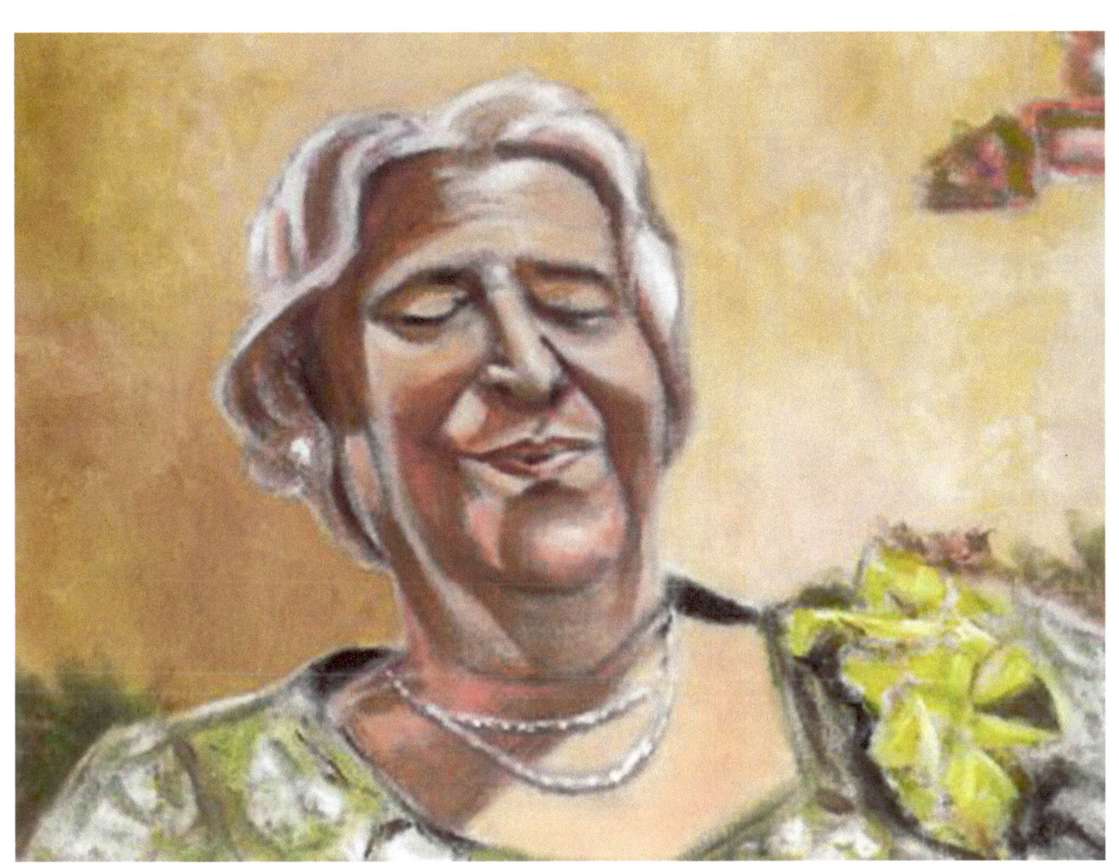

MIA NONA MARIA ANTONIO

My Nona, my father's mother, Maria Antonio, was born in Naples, Italy. She lived in a town called Torre del Greco at the base of Mt. Vesuvius. She would often say how difficult it was living with an active volcano in her backyard. She would talk about the eruptions. The town remained there because the soil was very fertile. She came to the United States in about 1900.

I loved visiting with her on Sundays. Italian music was always playing in her kitchen. After Mass, she made her famous homemade pasta, tagliolini. She would roll out the dough, then cut it into strips that looked like egg noodles. Then she would place a clean sheet on her bed, where she would keep the strips of pasta covered in flour until just before dinner. It is still my favorite pasta. In addition to being a great cook, she was very religious. In her bedroom she had an altar on her dresser, where a candle was always lit. Nona will always be a saint to me.

In this painting, she is standing in front of my Aunt Madeline's house in Flatbush, Brooklyn. I liked going to her house because it was close to the ocean. My father would go clamming and crabbing when we went to Madeline's house.

My parents spoke Italian when they didn't want us to know what they were saying. Nona only spoke a Neapolitan dialect of Italian. I remember when I went to high school and wanted to study Italian, the teacher, Mrs. Scaffuro, asked, "Does anyone in this class speak Italian?" I raised my hand, and she asked me how to say "What is your name?" I said, "Gome se gama." She said, "It is 'come si chiama.' Now don't say another word until you learn correct Italian." I studied Italian for three years. I love the language and Italian traditions.

I also remember holidays like Christmas, especially Christmas Eve. My father's whole family gathered for the feast. Being Neapolitan, we always had fish on the menu. We celebrated the traditional Feast of the Seven Fishes. My mother learned all of my grand-mother's recipes, so even after Nona's death we continued the tradition. I keep it to this day. It is my favorite meal.

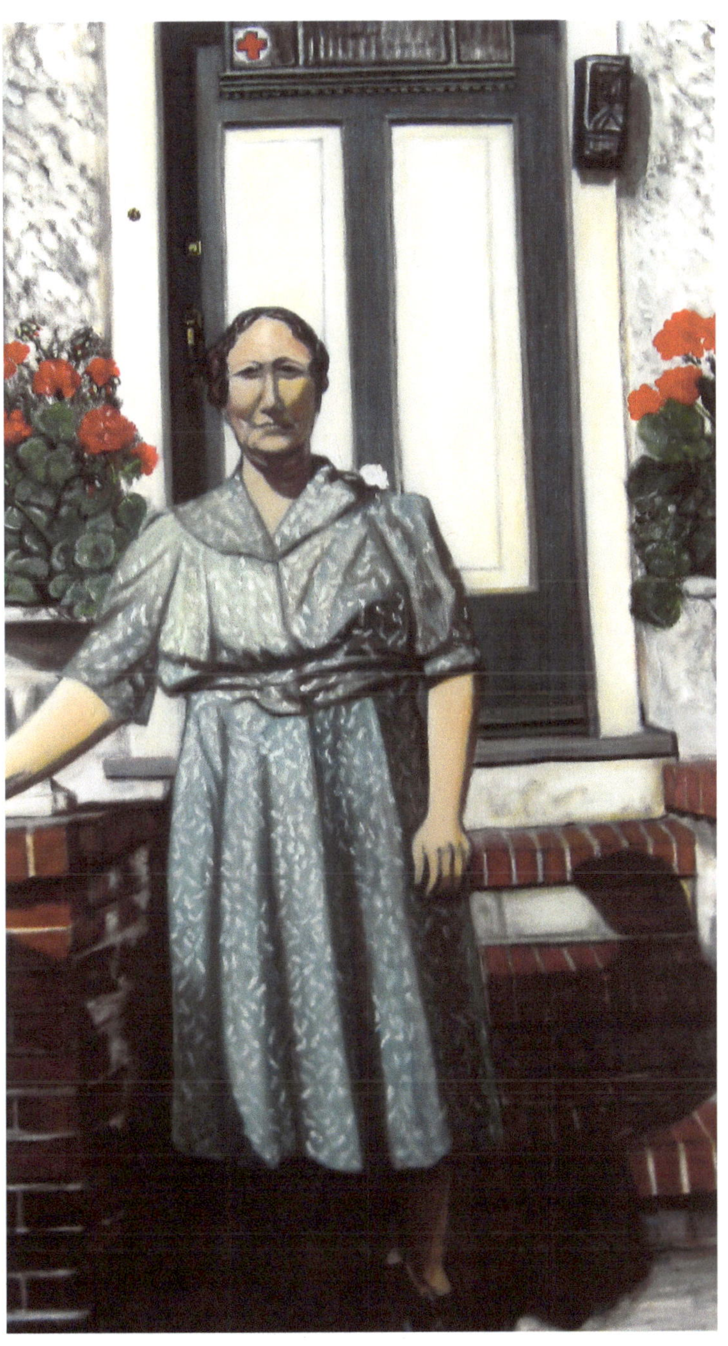

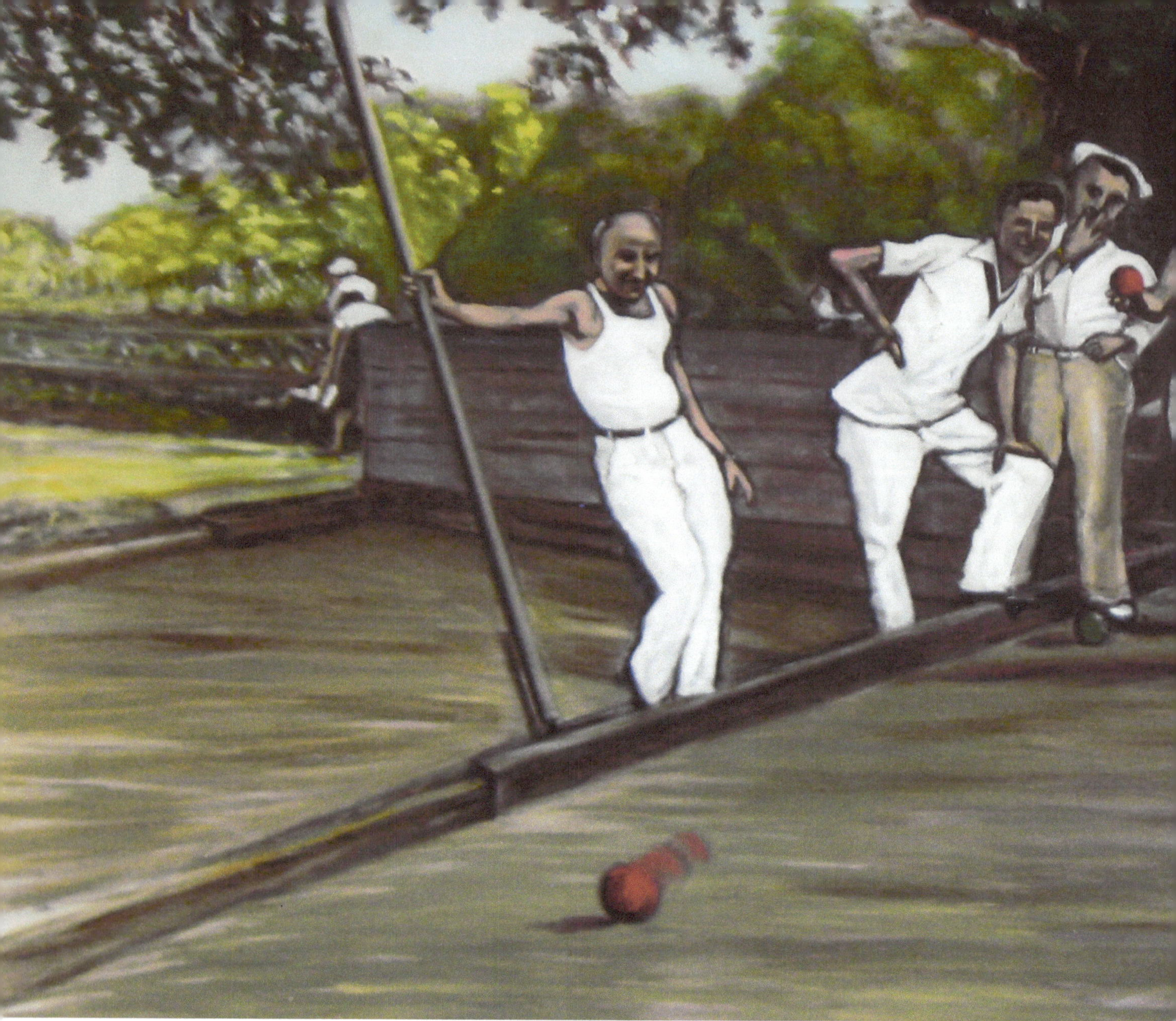

BOCCE Here's an Italian story that bocce players will love. In this painting we see my father leaning up against the back wall of the bocce court watching his friends play. The fat man to his left smoking the cigarette is my uncle Alfred, my father's brother-in-law.

I think they were playing bocce somewhere on Long Island's north shore. I found the original photo that I used for this painting in one of my father's drawers one day. I don't know who took the original picture, but I sure love the composition. You couldn't compose a

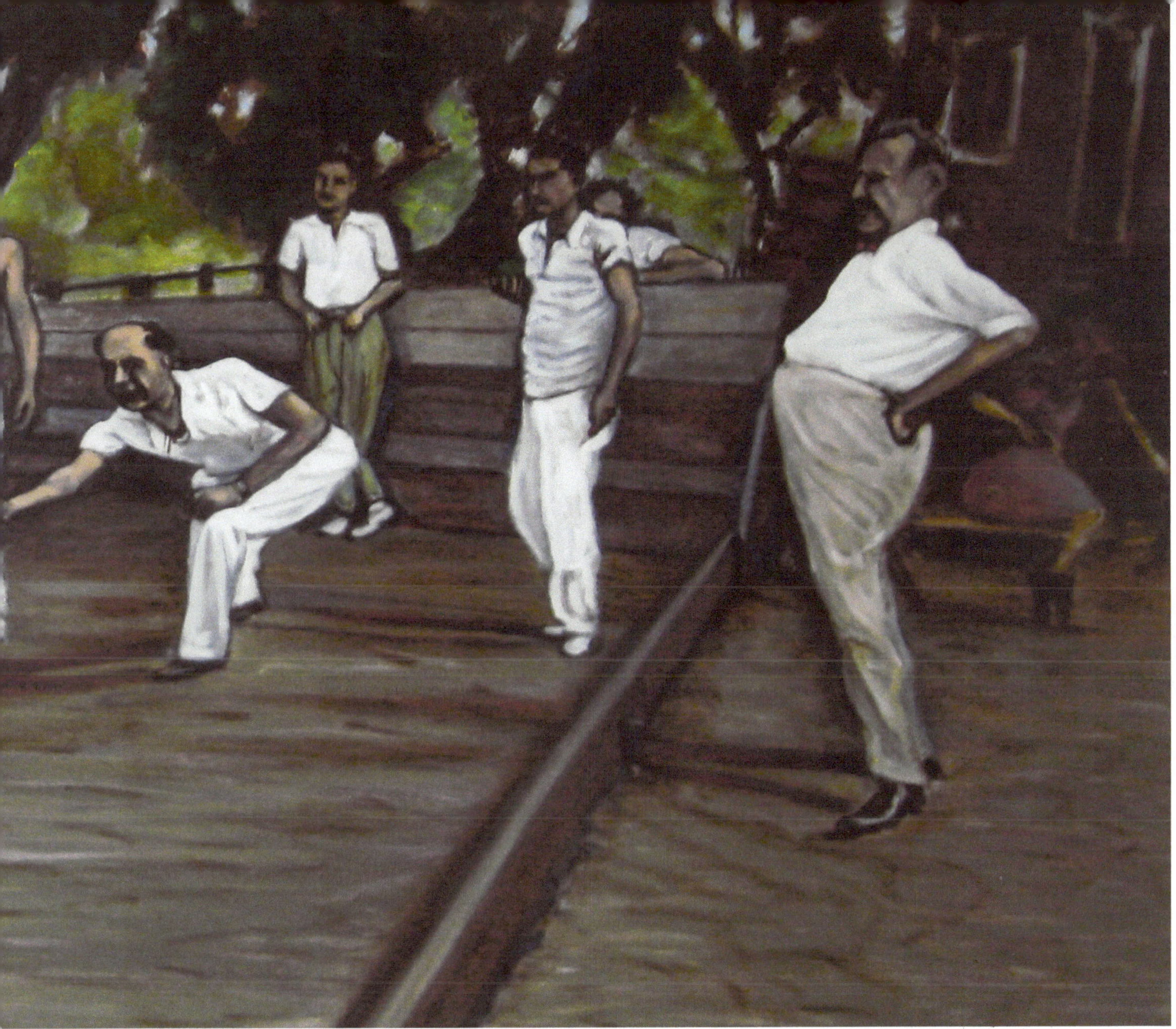

picture like this if you tried. It was a perfect accident. It captures a scene so common among young Italian men.

The picture had to be taken sometime in the late 1930s or early 1940s. I love the two women all the way to the left; they seem to be gardening. There is a guy—probably one of my father's friends—leaning over his shoulder, and you can see the large breasts of another woman under the elbow of the young sailor.

MY PARENTS COURTING, PROSPECT PARK

This painting is of my parents courting in Prospect Park, Brooklyn. The year was 1937 or 1938. They were married in 1939.

The trees in the background look rather young. The park was recently renovated. My mother is all dressed up and so is my father, in his pinstripe suit. He loved wearing a hat. I remember that he would always place it back in its box when he wasn't wearing it. What a good-looking couple they made.

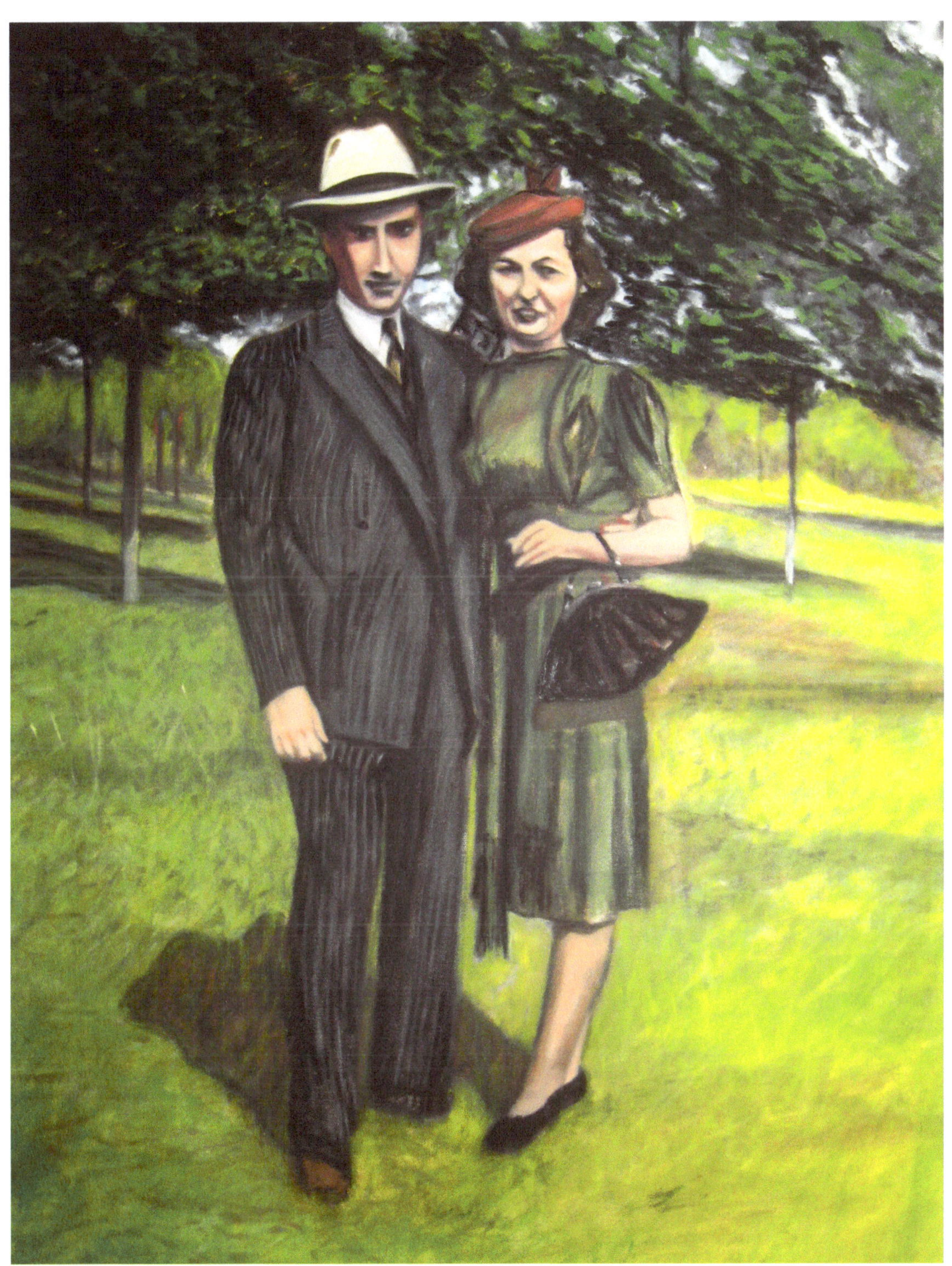

MY PARENTS' WEDDING

The year was 1939. The date was February 12—President Lincoln's birthday. The place was Carroll Street, Brooklyn, New York. The church was Our Lady of Peace. My father was 24 years old, and my mother was 22. That's when my parents were married. The background is very art deco and so is the style.

As I was painting the train on my mother's gown, I couldn't help feeling that their entire future together lay beneath it. Needless to say, I got very wound up in it.

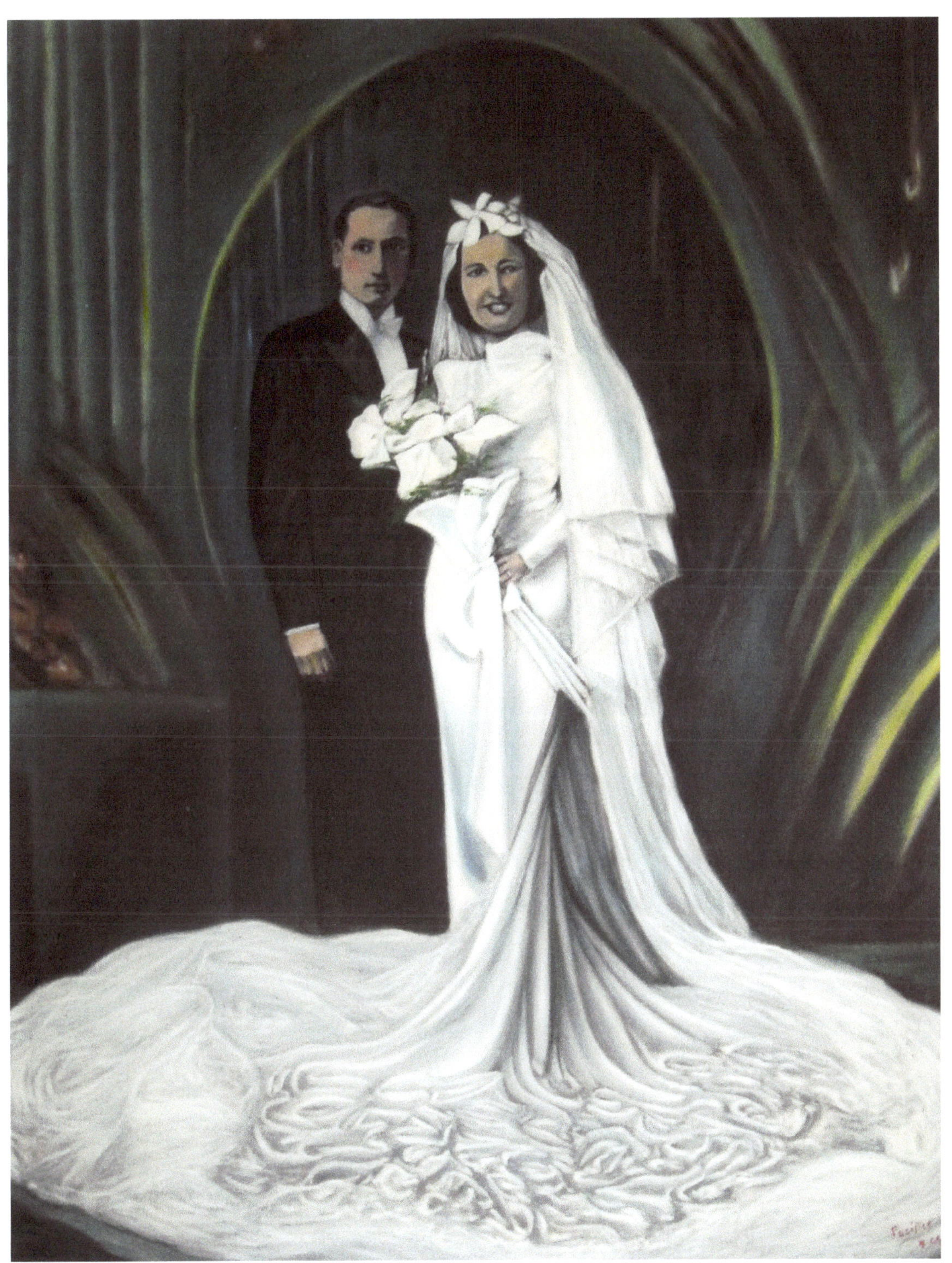

MY BROTHER MICHAEL

My brother Michael was born January 31, 1943. He was named after my mother's father. He was born on the date of my grandfather's death. He was afraid of the dog when the photographer took the picture this painting is based on.

Today, Michael lives in Taiwan. He is a teacher and holds a doctorate in Italian history. He's written several books on history.

And he's still afraid of dogs.

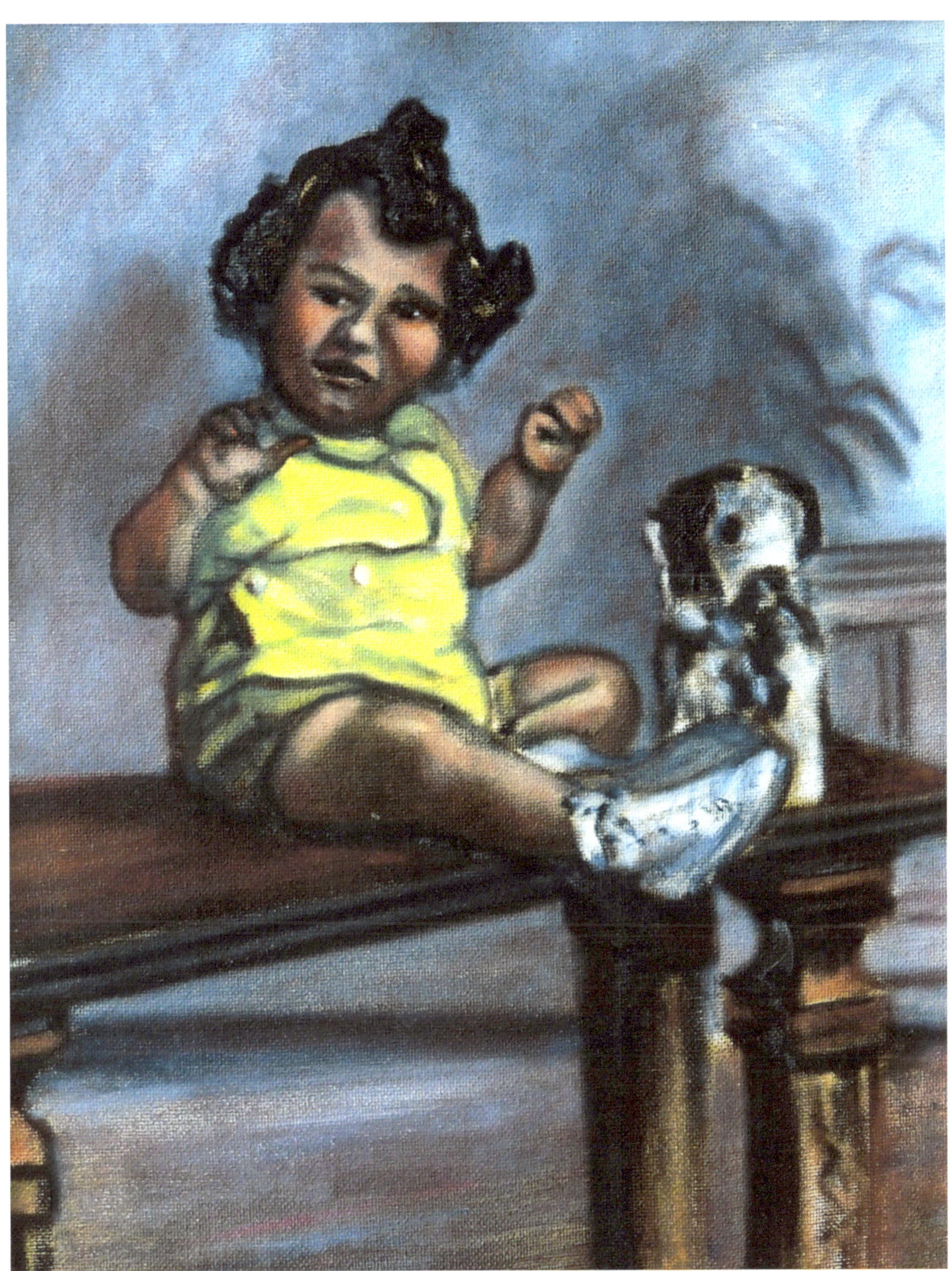

PROSPECT PARK CAROUSEL

What goes around comes around. I don't really remember the day it happened I only saw the picture. It was me sitting on one of the horses. When I was old enough I went there to see it for myself. It was beautiful watching the horses going up and down and people reaching for the golden ring. If you were lucky enough to catch one, you could ride again for free.

I'm not sure if the carousel is still there anymore. If it isn't, it would be a big loss.

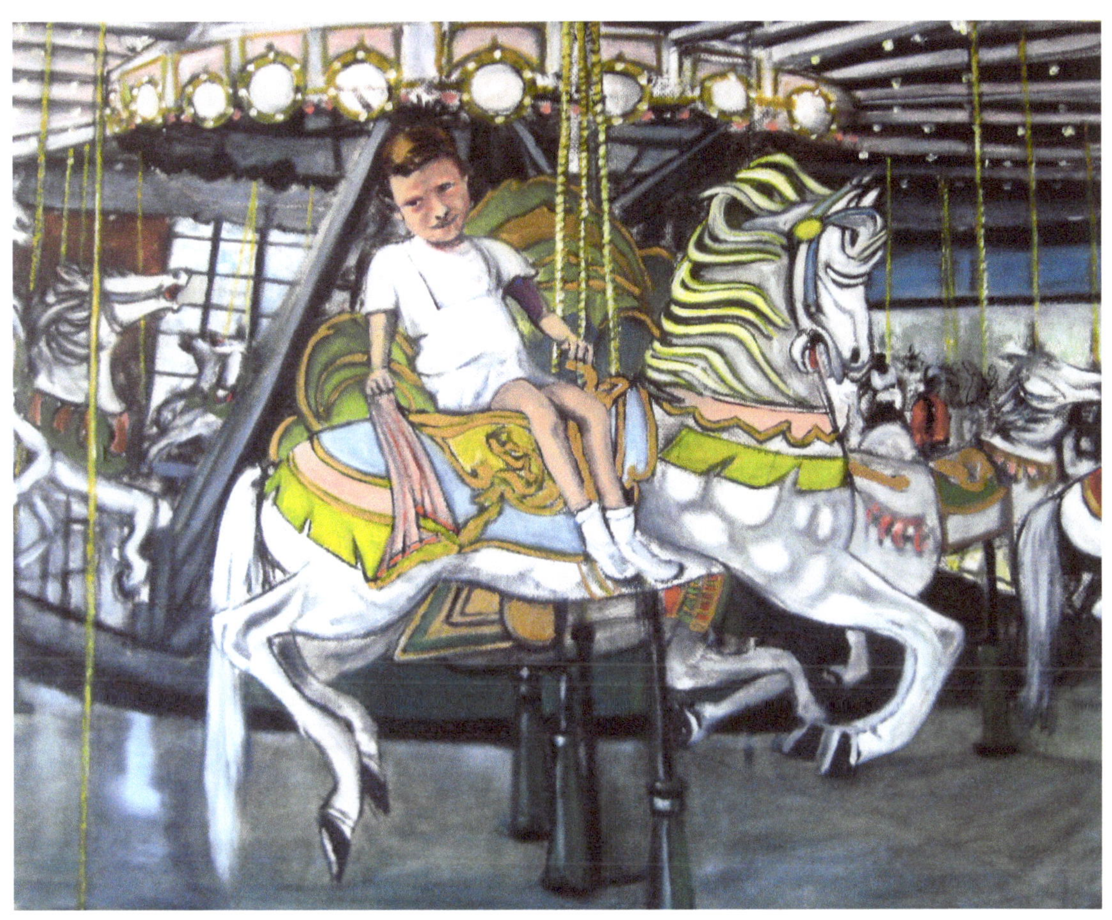

UNCLE TONY'S BARBER SHOP

I think my Aunt Tessie took the photo that inspired this painting. I found a similar picture of Aunt Tessie and me taken on the same day with me holding her hand, so I assume she took this of me holding my father's hand in front of my Uncle Tony's barber shop. In the window, you can see reflections of the apartment buildings that lined the street across from the shop.

This must have been in late 1942 or early 1943. The war was going on, and patriotism was running high in neighborhoods everywhere. Here, Uncle Sam and the American flag figure prominently.

My aunt snapped this photo around Easter time. I remember how hot it was. I was wearing an outfit that my mother had picked out for me, probably from Erwin's. She loved to shop there around Easter time and buy me and my brother a new jacket or suit. I held my father's hand, crossed my foot and looked at the camera as my aunt took the picture. Look at all the old posters and signs that were on the wall behind me. Look at the old Penny Scale up against the wall of the barber shop.

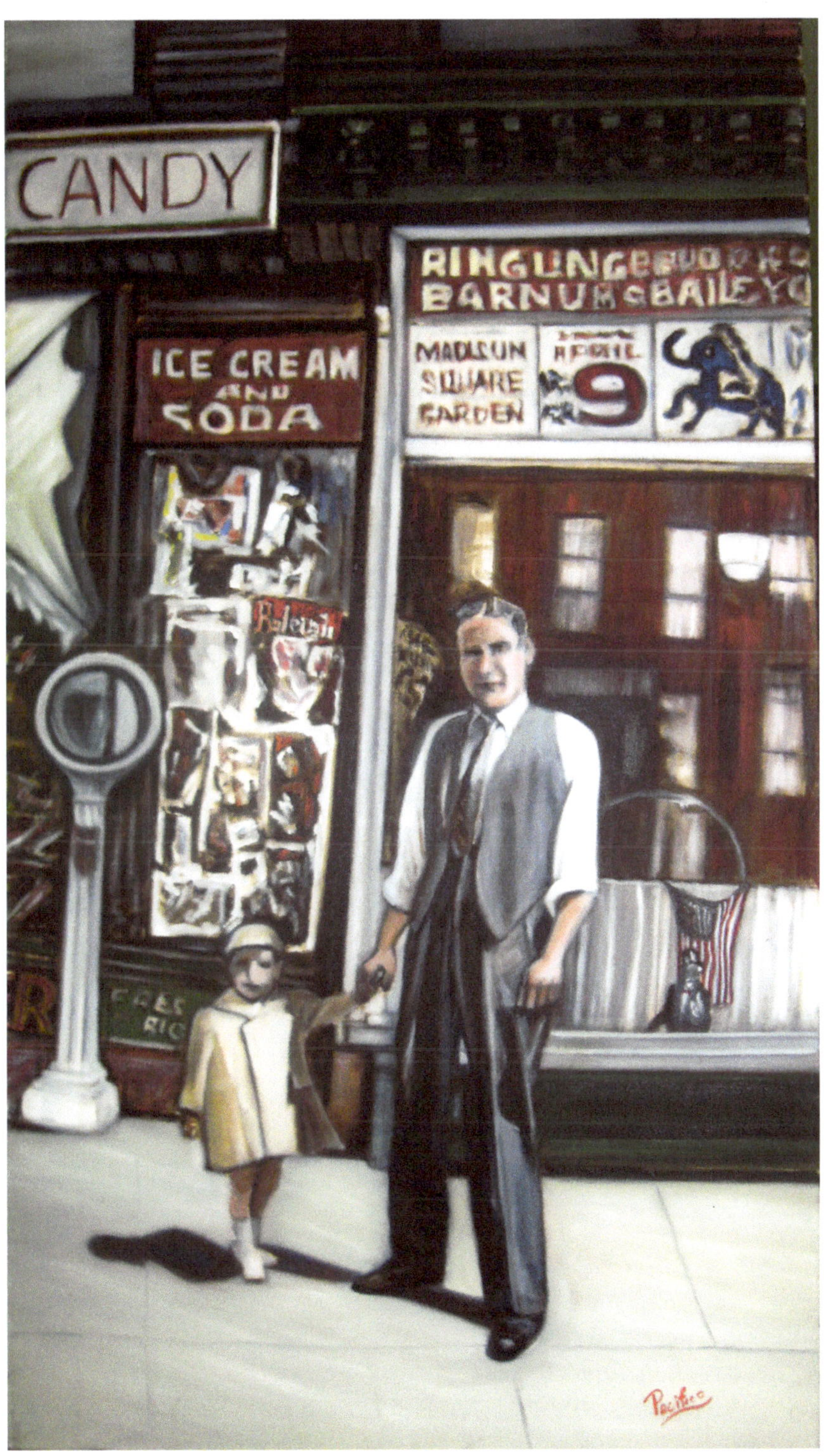
CANDY
ICE CREAM AND SODA
Raleigh

STATUE OF LIBERTY

What I remember most about the Statue of Liberty was going there. My father took my brother and me to see her. We went by ferry. It was my first time on a ferry. We seemed to be so high above the water. I remember the ferry starting up to move. I was leaning against the railing looking down into the water. Suddenly this huge amount of foam stirred beneath us. It was scary at first. Then we moved out. I could see the statue in the distance. As we got closer she began to get bigger and bigger.

I couldn't believe how big she was. My father asked a man to take a picture of us in front of her. Then we walked up the stairs and it seemed to take forever to reach the top. Looking down from the torch, I could see Liberty's beautiful smiling face that seemed to be staring up at us. Then I looked around and saw the ships passing in the water below us. I will always remember the day. And I think often of the Lady in the Harbor smiling as she welcomes the newcomers to our wonderful country, and how much she means to us. It makes me cry when I think of how my grandparents must have felt the first time they saw her.

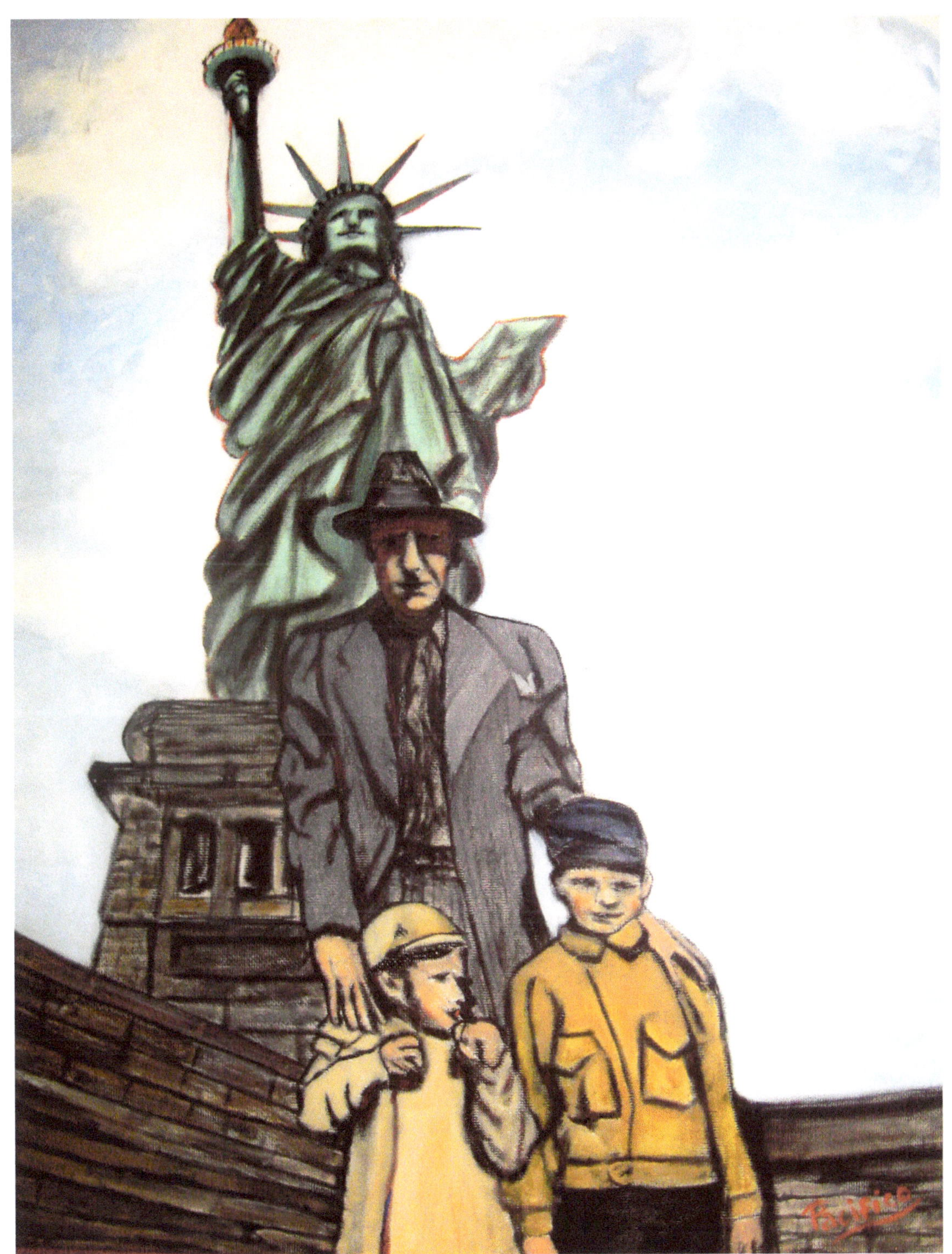

VESUVIO BAKERY

Before my father bought our brownstone on Carroll Street in Park Slope we lived on Fifth Avenue between Carroll and Garfield streets. Our apartment was above a bread store called Guarino's. Vesuvio was located in Manhattan and I painted it because it looked very much like Guarino's. They baked the best Italian, French, and Sicilian bread around.

We got the smell of fresh bread baking all day long. If my father turned on his exhaust fan, the incoming air smelled so fantastic. My father would walk down the stairs and buy a fresh loaf to make his sandwich at 6 a.m. I got my bread for lunch when I came home from school at noon. Then my mother bought another fresh loaf for dinner. In the late '40s and early '50s, the prices were 7 cents for a small loaf, 12 cents for a medium loaf, and 15 cents for a large one. There were all kinds of breads to choose from. At Easter and Christmas they baked special breads and biscotti. We soaked the hard biscotti in tomato sauce, especially for scurgill, shrimp and clam sauce.

My mother did all her shopping within a one-block radius. Downstairs to our left was Millers, a great German bakery. I remember they made the best cream cakes and buns, with crumb, cheese, lemon, and jelly to choose. Next to Guarino's was Pipitones Butcher Store. On the opposite corner was Patsy's Solumeria. On the other corner was Cioffes Pastceria. They made wonderful Italian pastries and in the summer I loved their lemon ice. In the street, peddlers passed by in horse-drawn carts. A little old man or lady would walk up to the horses carrying an empty valise. They placed the open valise directly under the horse's tail and waited. After the horse went, they closed the valise and carried the droppings home to their garden. I thought that was very funny.

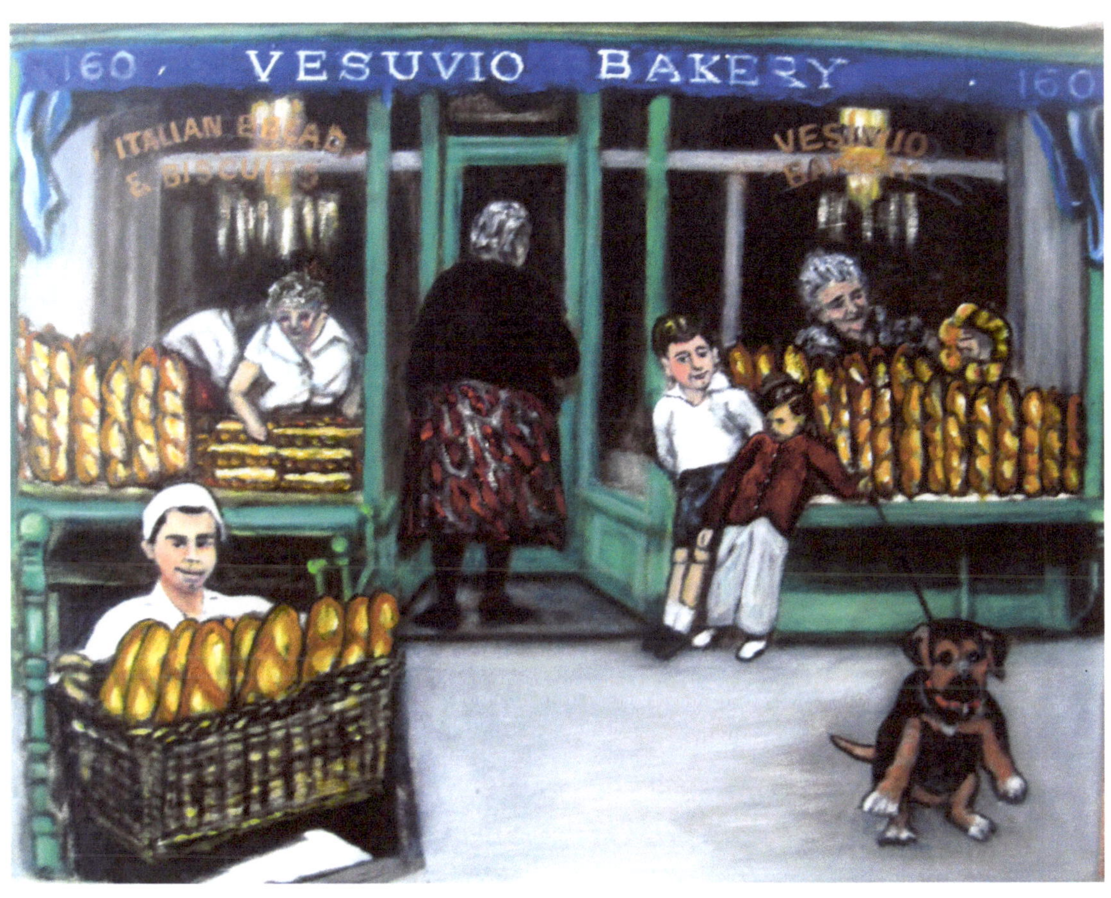
160
VESUVIO BAKERY
160

ALLY POND PARK

My parents loved to go on picnics. One of our favorite places was Alley Pond State Park. I especially enjoyed the sliding pond. It had four ladders going at one time and four slides. My father loved it because he enjoyed swimming and so did I. It seemed like everybody went there. I'm the one with the red bathing suit. My father is holding my brother, and the little boy next to me is Donnie, a neighbor from our apartment house.

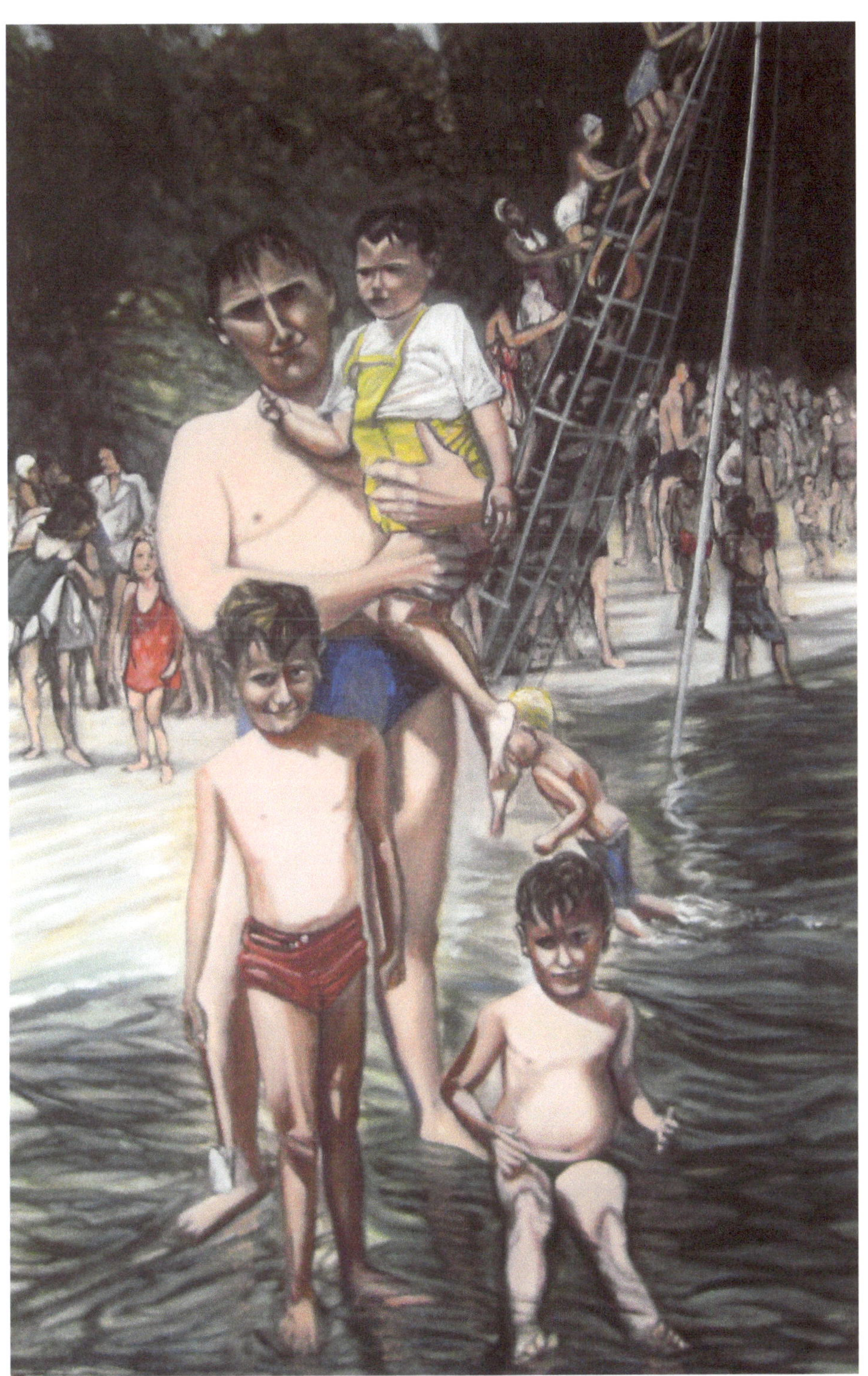

CARVEL

There was a Carvel store close to where we lived in Brooklyn. We would go there often in the summer. My parents would take my brother and me there at night after dinner.

I liked chocolate and my brother wanted vanilla. I loved the lights and especially the neon Carvel sign.

The funny thing is when I moved to Massachusetts from New York, I didn't know what soft serve was. What is that?

We called it custard in New York

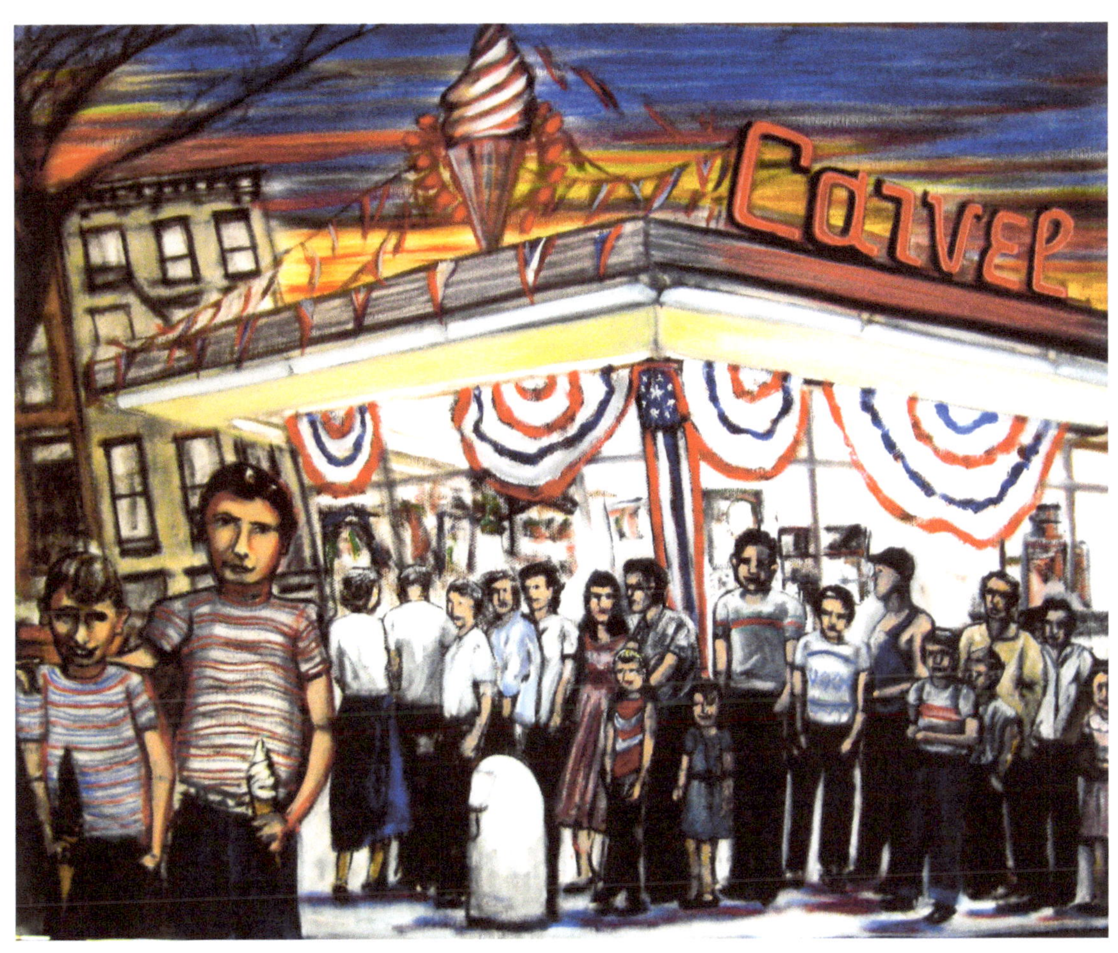
Carvel

THE CHEF. MICHAEL COLLINS

My Italian story has some Irish-English mixed in it too. That's where Michael enters the picture.

The painting below was inspired by a photo of him in a sailor suit, which was taken in a department store in Queens, New York. I like the suit.

The one on the facing page was inspired from a photo taken by friends at their home in Vermont.

Ours is a long story and a good story, but too long to be told in this book. It's almost 55 years long right now. We just hope that it can continue for a long long time.

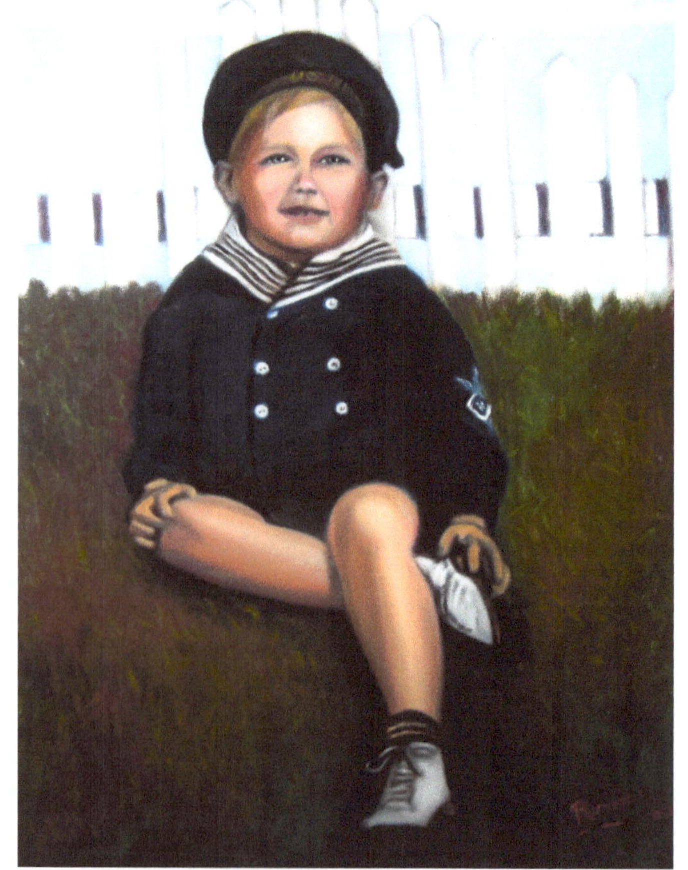

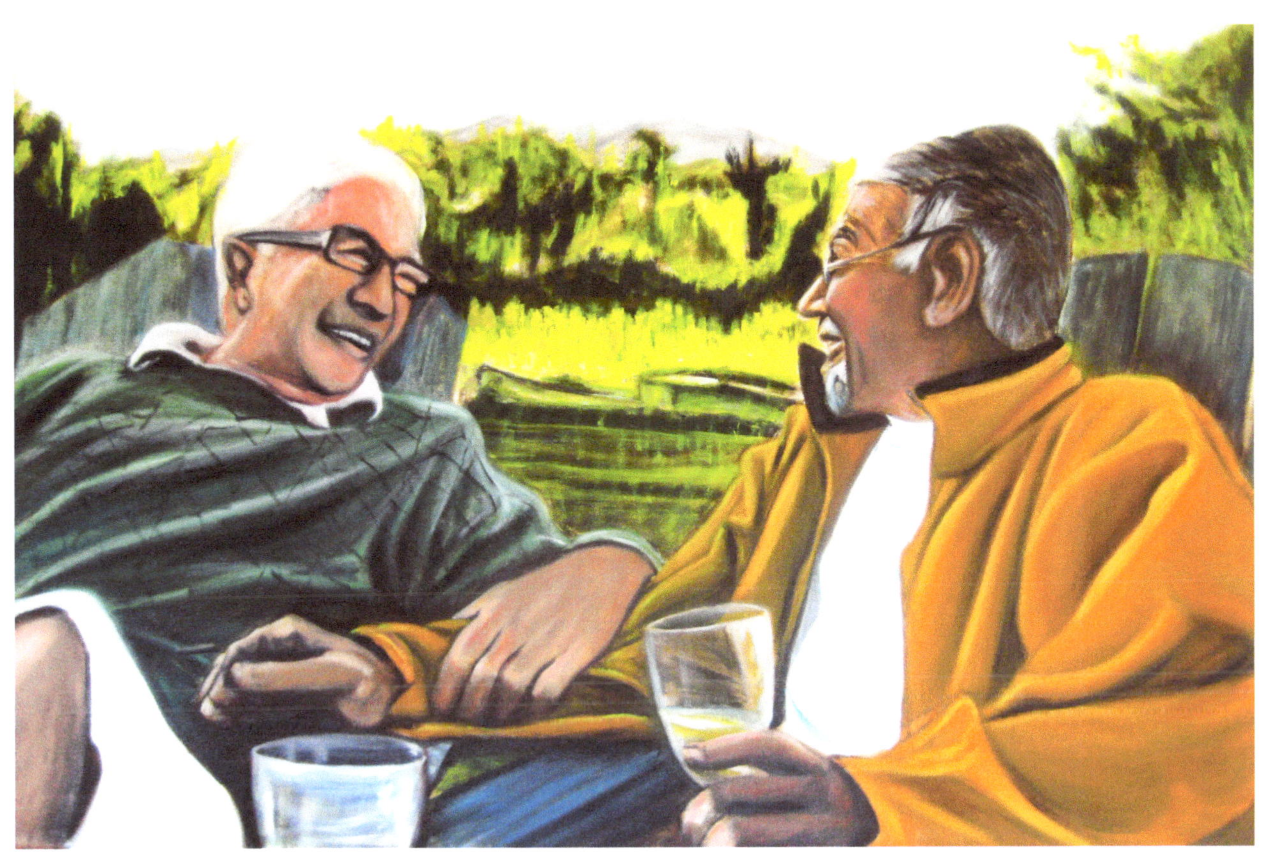

AUNT HELEN

It's difficult to explain how I felt as I painted this portrait of my Aunt Helen. Before I started painting it, I stared at the blank canvas and at the photo that Michael, my partner, had taken of her. I said, "Aunt Helen I want you to come through to me, I want to show you as you are."

She was a very kind person. She worked very hard. During the work week, her "scoffer" as she called him, would drive her and several other men and woman out to Maspeth, Long Island. She worked for The National Can Company. She pressed cans all day long. That's why she had such big hands. As I began to paint her, I began to cry. I cried for a half-hour. That's how long it took me to paint her. Then I put my brush down.

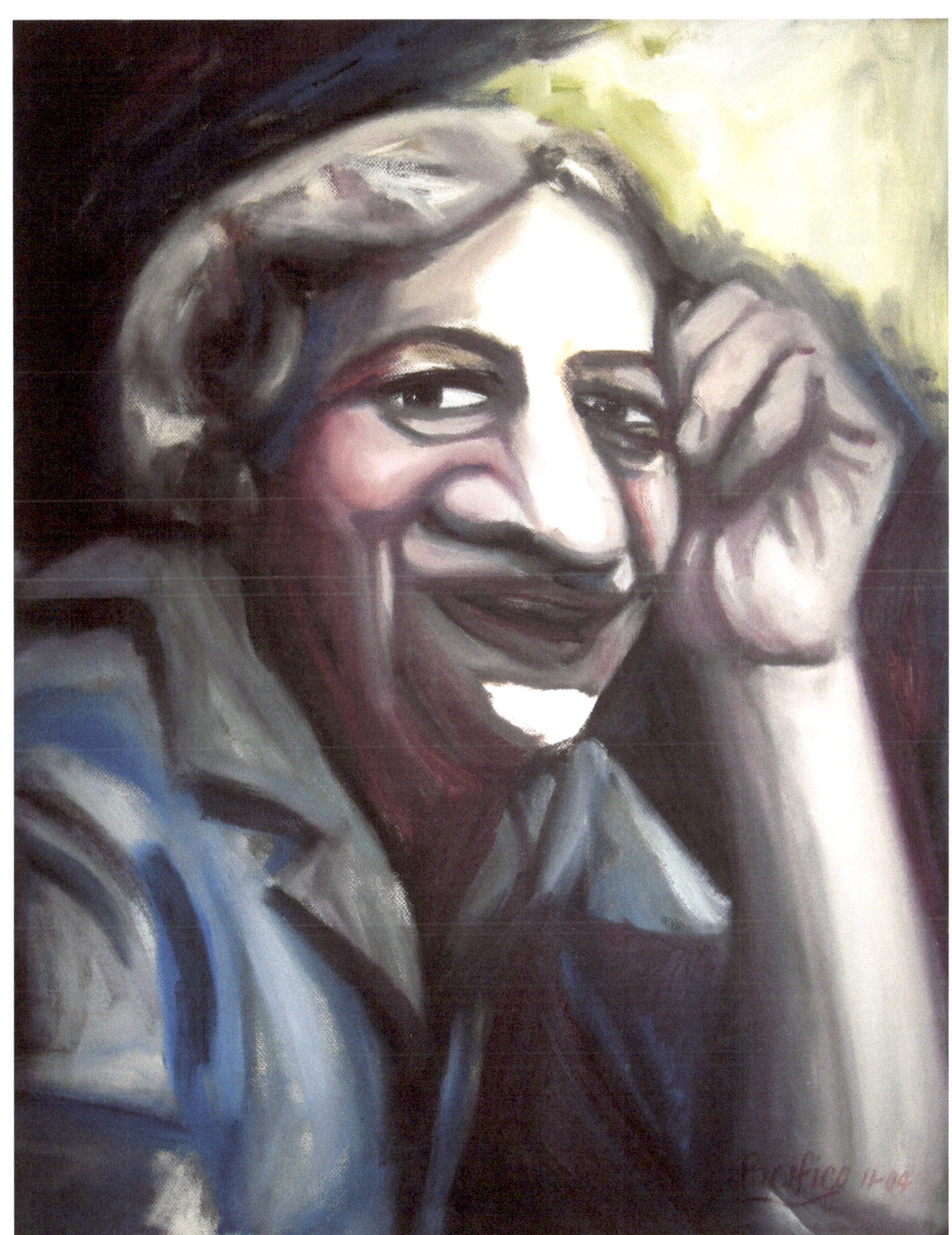

MY FIRST HOLY COMMUNION

This is me receiving my First Holy Communion. Jesus and the angel were painted in the backdrop after the picture was taken at the studio. I added the clouds and the cypress trees in the style of van Gogh—another one of my favorite artists.

I remember that morning. In those days, you weren't supposed to eat before receiving Communion. I forgot about fasting and before the ceremony, I went downstairs to Millers, the bakery shop below our apartment, and bought three vanilla cupcakes and ate them.

As I entered the church that morning, I didn't know what to do—should I receive Communion or not? I chose to receive.

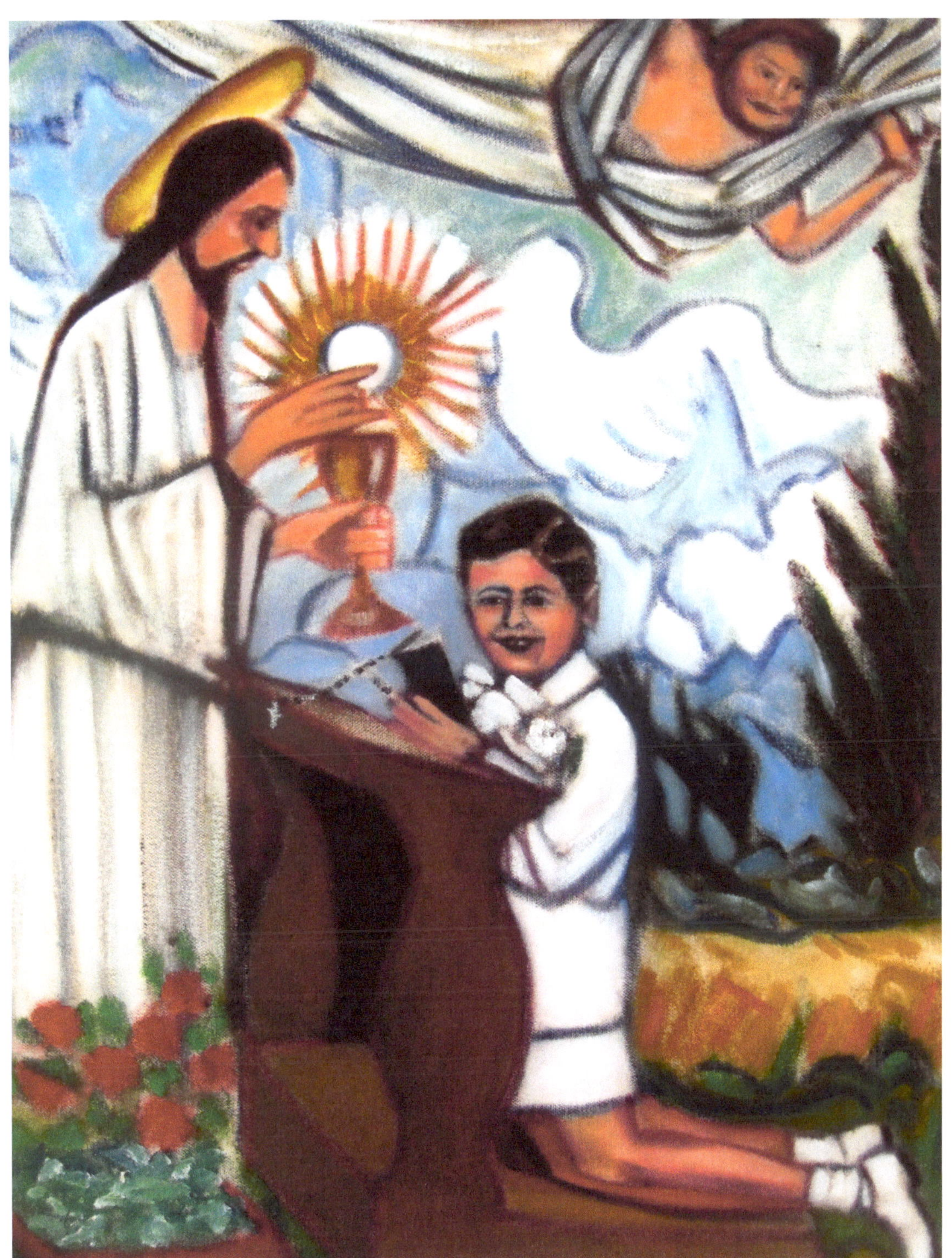

BROOKLYN BRIDGE

Before I created this painting, I kept thinking, why does the Brooklyn Bridge mean so much to me? Is it because I was born in Brooklyn?

Then I discovered the picture of my parents with me on the bridge; they must have had someone take the picture. I would ride over the bridge by train and by car every time I went to New York. It was a huge part of our life.

In 1983, when the bridge turned 100 years old, the Brooklyn Museum held a contest to come up with an exciting way to show the bridge. Being a neon artist, I knew what I would do. I created a 48-inch sculpture of the bridge. I won the contest. My neon Brooklyn Bridge was displayed in the Brooklyn Museum for an entire year.

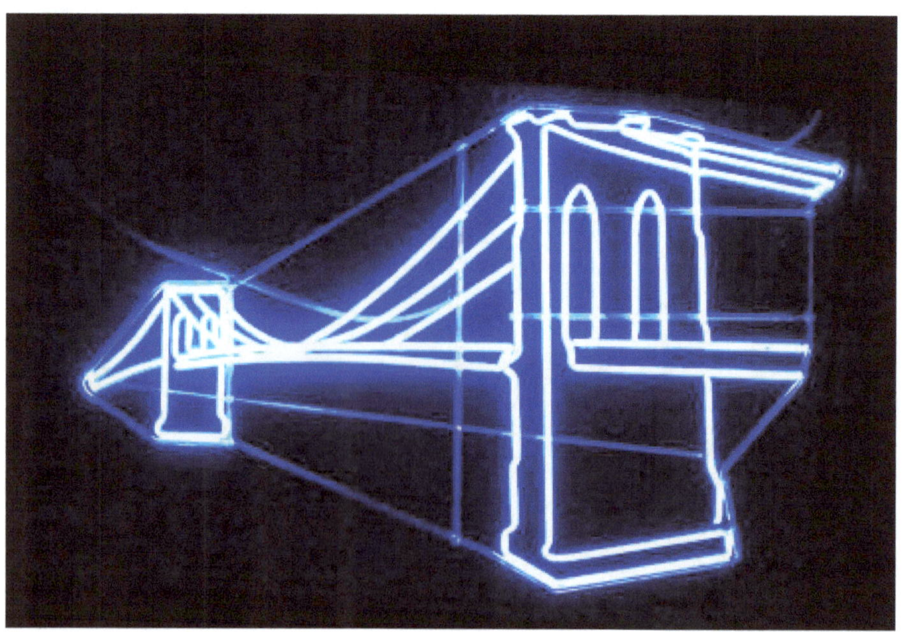

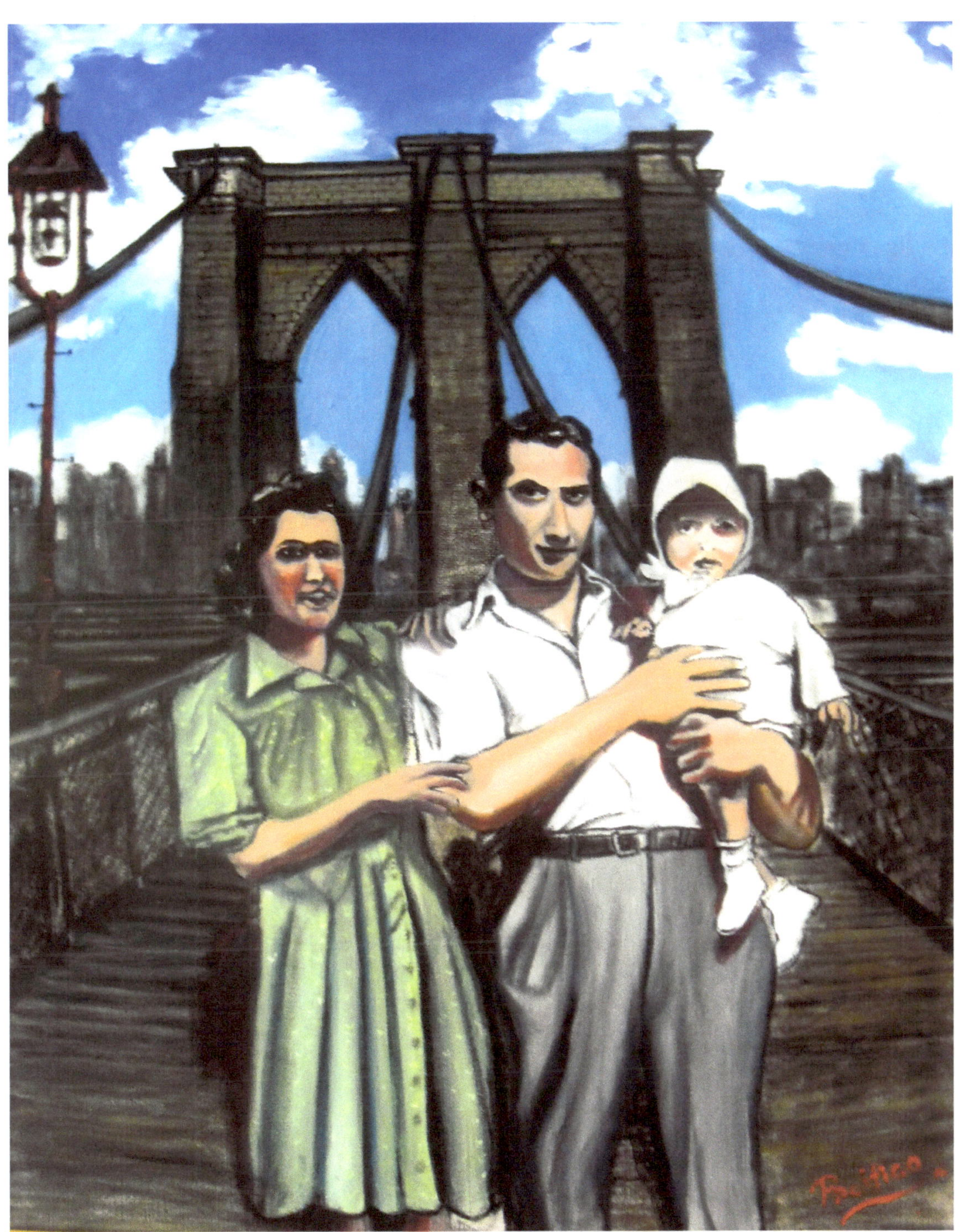

ENJOY YOURSELF

I was there the day this picture was taken. It was the Fourth of July. I'm sitting on the arm of the swing with my head down contemplating life, as I did in those days. My Uncle George is serenading his wife, my Fat Aunt Mary. If we didn't call her Fat Aunt Mary, she wouldn't talk to us.

She would come to my mother's house in the mornings and beg her for something to eat. She thought nothing of eating a steak for breakfast. She would say, "When I die and they put me in a coffin, I'm going to get my money's worth."

I remember the day like it was yesterday. We were at my Uncle Jack and Aunt Rosie's house enjoying the day. My uncle is the man on the left drinking beer; Aunt Rosie, my grandmother's other sister, is on the right, in the pink dress. My father, in the striped polo shirt, is singing along with everyone else. The song was "Enjoy Yourself. It's Later Than You Think." That song and "Sweet Violets" were Aunt Mary's favorite songs. They're all gone now. Except for me—

Enjoy yourself, it's later than you think
Enjoy yourself while you're still in the pink
The years go by as quickly as a wink
Enjoy yourself, enjoy yourself
It's later than you think

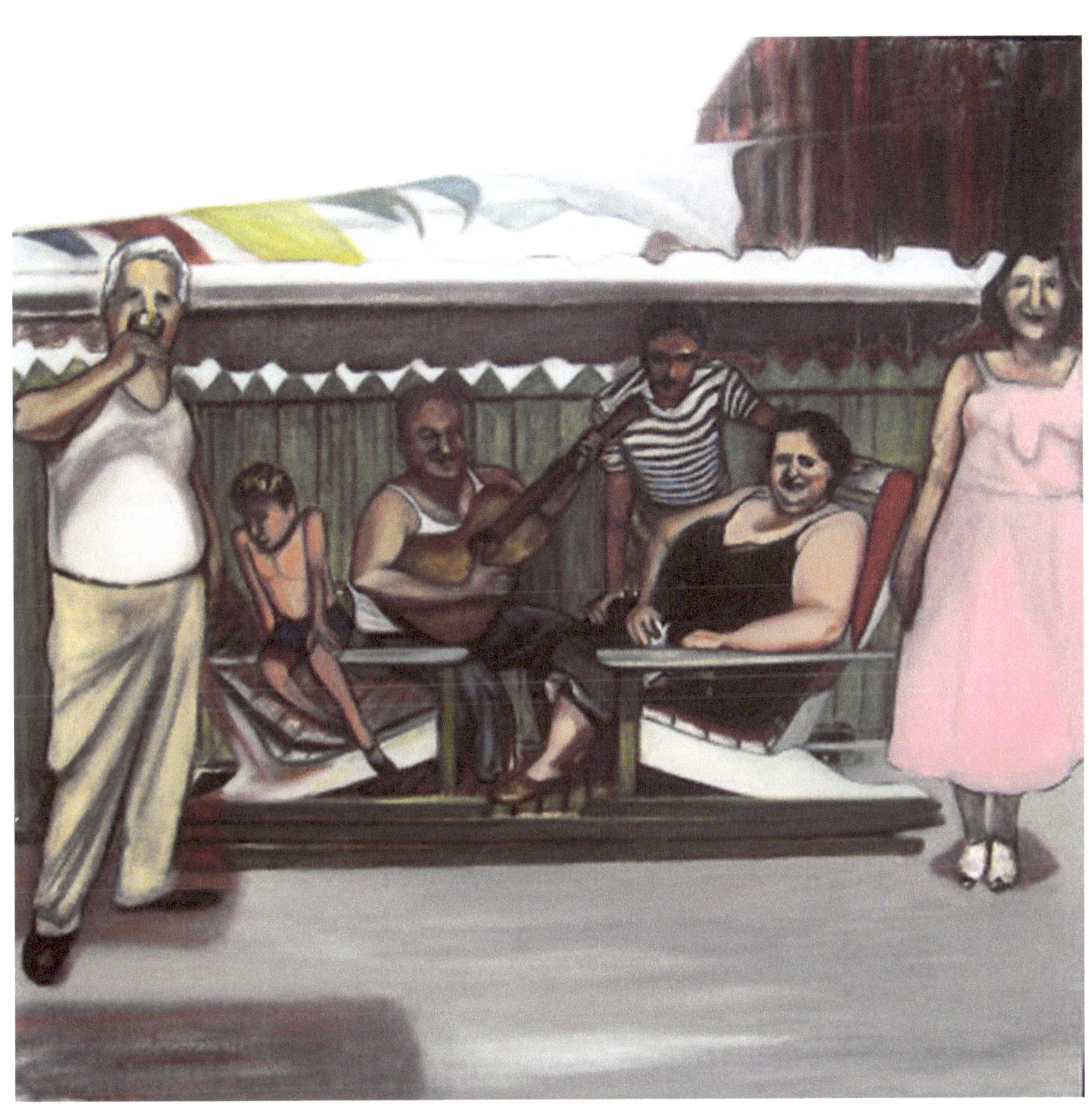

AUNT MINNIE'S WEDDING

After my grandfather died, my grandmother remarried the widower Mr. Ponzi, who lived across the street from her. We called him Pappy.

He had two children, Minnie and Chick. When Minnie was married, I was the little flower boy, in the front of the painting. Next to me is Lucille, who lived across the street from Aunt Minnie. Lucille was born the day after me, on April 5, 1941.

Behind me is Aunt Lola, who was the maid of honor. To her left is her husband, my Uncle Phillie. Then there is Aunt Minnie, the bride, looking radiant. To her right is Pappy. The man all the way in the back is my Uncle Freddie.

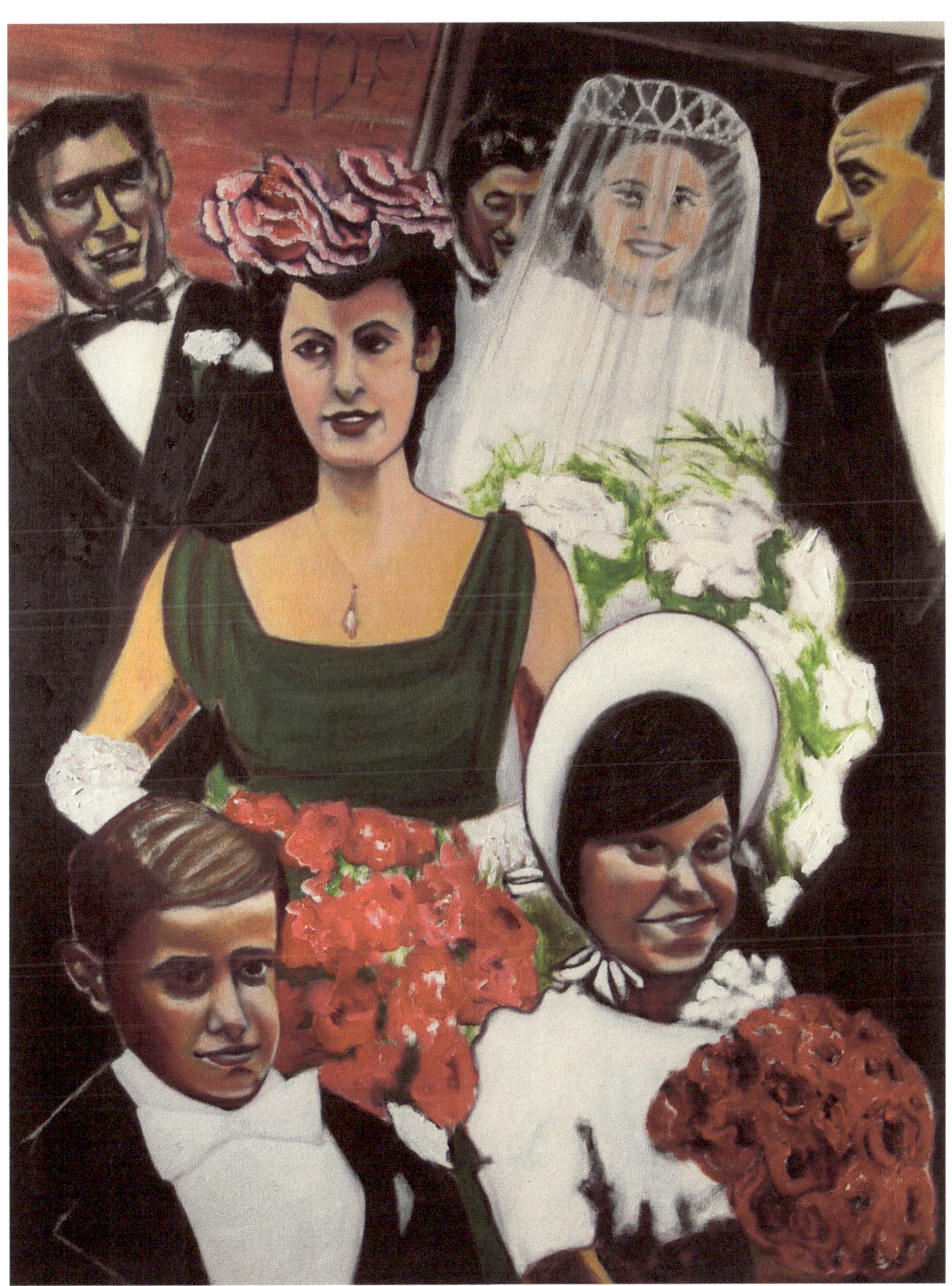

AUNT LOLA'S ENGAGEMENT

My cousin Susan sent me the original photo of my Aunt Lola's engagement. I loved the photo from the moment I saw it.

The year was probably about 1944, maybe 1945. Here's Aunt Lola, who was probably about 20 or 21 at the time, dressed so beautifully with pearls in her hair. I decided on the green dress and the pink roses on her hip.

Next to her is Pappy, my step-grandfather. Aunt Lola seems to be playing up to him. She always liked teasing him. Next to her is Grandma, in her red (again I decided that) sequin gown, smiling.

And next to her is my Uncle Philly. Doesn't he look sharp and a little sinister? He thought that he was Clark Gable. I think he had just returned from the army. The setting is his father's Italian restaurant, Villa Antico, in Brooklyn. I especially love the wallpaper.

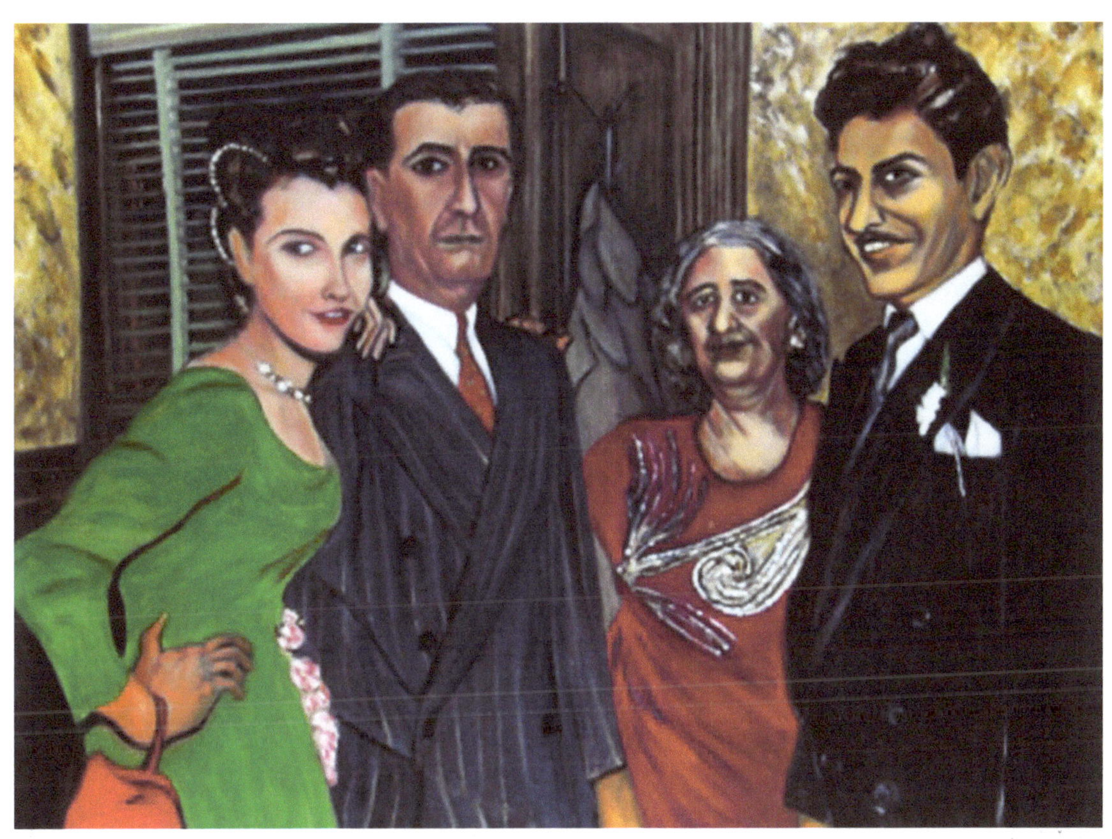

AUNT TESSIE AT LOLA'S ENGAGEMENT

I was so taken by the photograph of my Aunti Tessie entering the room to join Aunt Lola's engagement party. You see the flash going off as she pulls aside the curtain.

It seemed like a natural Edward Hopper setting to me. I just had to paint it. I hope you enjoy it.

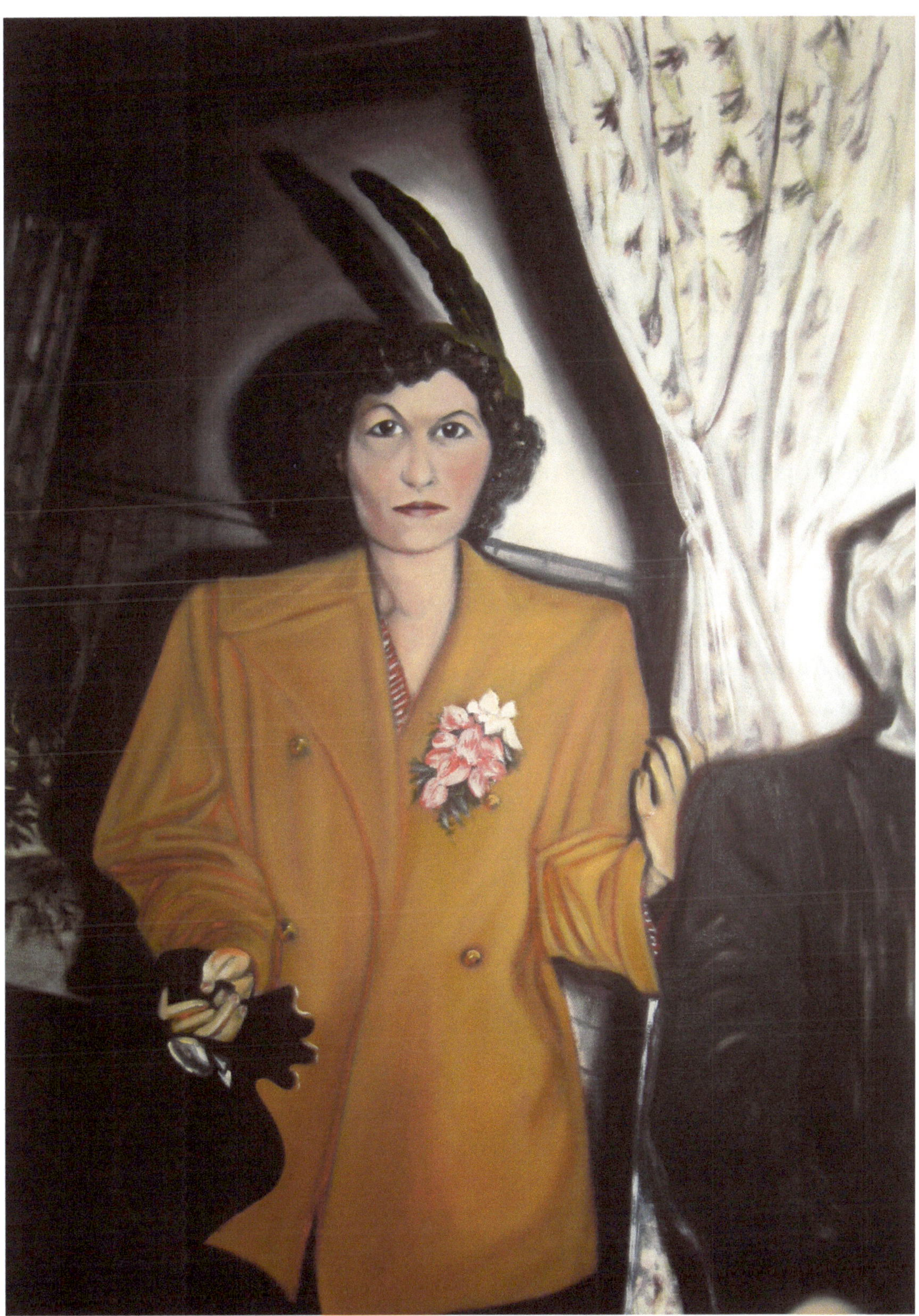

AUNT LOLA'S WEDDING

I remember bits and pieces of this day. Mostly, I remember the excitement. It was Aunt Lola's wedding day. My mother looked beautiful as we walked to the church, Our Lady of Peace, a block from my grandmother's apartment.

My parents are walking together; I had my finger in my mouth as I held my father's hand. I love my mother's big black hat. To my mother's left is Aunt Tessie, my mother's youngest sister. She looks great in her red dress.

Behind us are my father's sisters. I recognize Aunt Julia, with her hair in curlers, walking with her son Anthony. Behind her is my Aunt Rossie. They didn't dress up for the wedding itself. The wedding was on my mother's side of the family. They dressed in the evening for the reception. Back then, it seemed as if the entire neighborhood turned out to see the wedding.

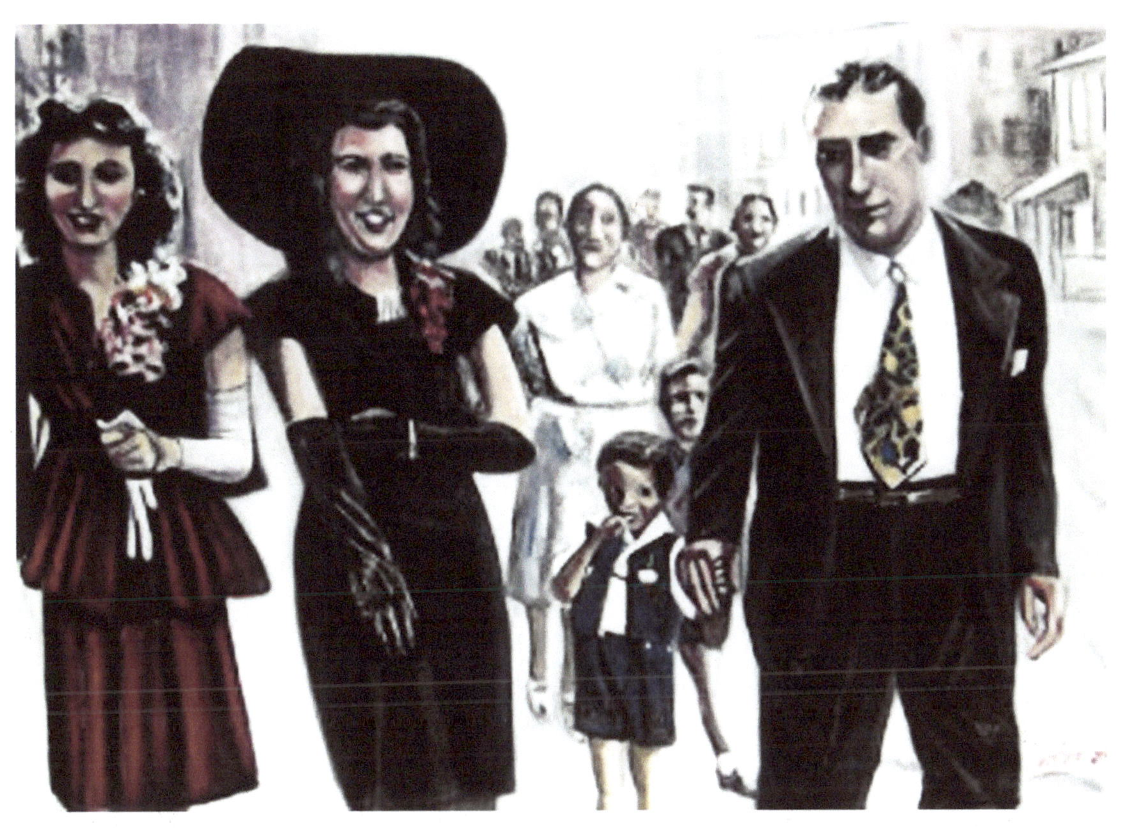

COUSIN SUSAN PLAYING GUITAR

Susan is my Aunt Lola's daughter. She is the sister I never had. I always felt very close to her. I painted her with her guitar because she seemed very into it when she was younger, and I remember we liked listening to Neil Young songs. I recently gave her the painting.

My Aunt Lola always had Susan looking her best. At Easter, Lola would come to my parents' house to show off Susan and her brother, Philip, wearing their latest outfits. I loved to photograph how great they looked.

When I moved to Colrain, Massachusetts, Susan always enjoyed visiting my house. I'll never forget when she married her first husband, Robert. They asked if they could spend their honeymoon at our home in Colrain. They were there for three weeks and Michael and I didn't bother them once. Finally, I decided to come up and check on them. When I got there, I was greeted by all her friends. She had invited them up to join her and all were having a great old time. Today, she lives close by in Massachusetts, where she bought her own home and practices her career as a therapist. Now we can see each other more often and even spend holidays together, which makes us very happy because we love each other very much.

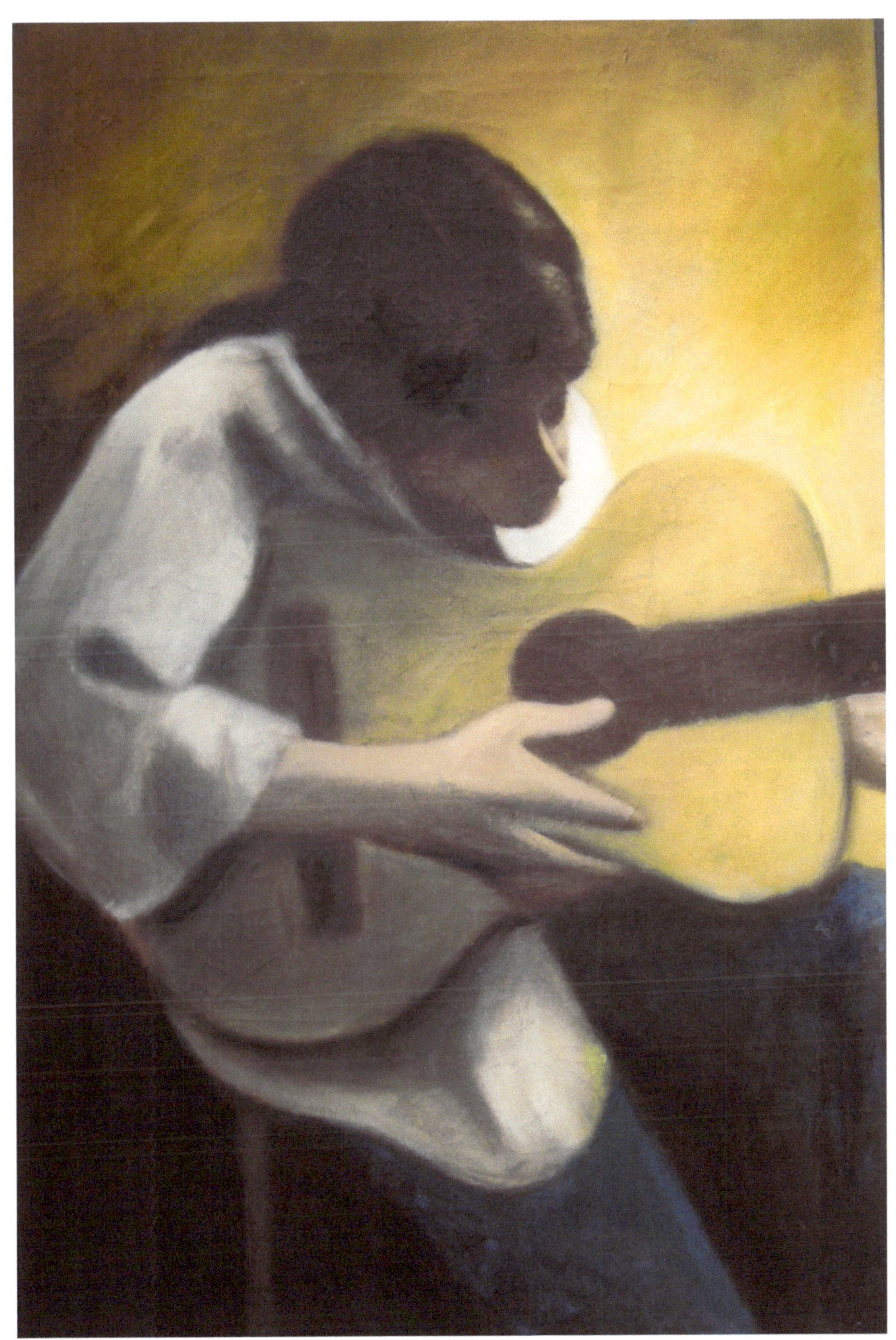

VALLEY STREAM PICNIC PARK

When my father bought his new '55 Chevy he loved to take us to Valley Stream Picnic Park. It was his pride and joy. He took this picture that I turned into a painting. He wanted to capture his new shining car. When he took the picture I started singing—*See the USA in Your Chevrolet.*

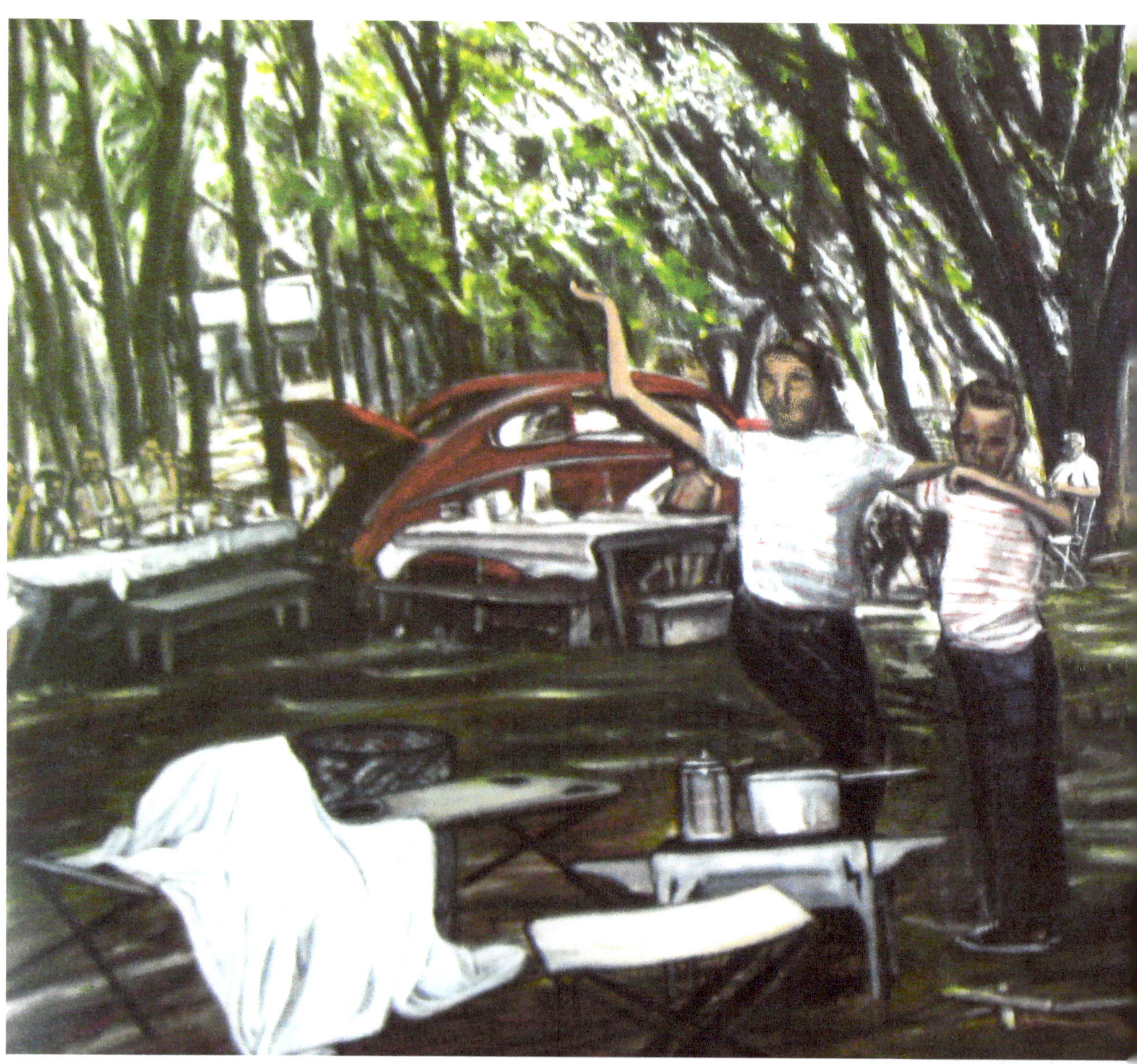

My brother wanted to rap me in the mouth. "Shut up shut up," he kept saying. Our mother just looked at my father as he took the picture

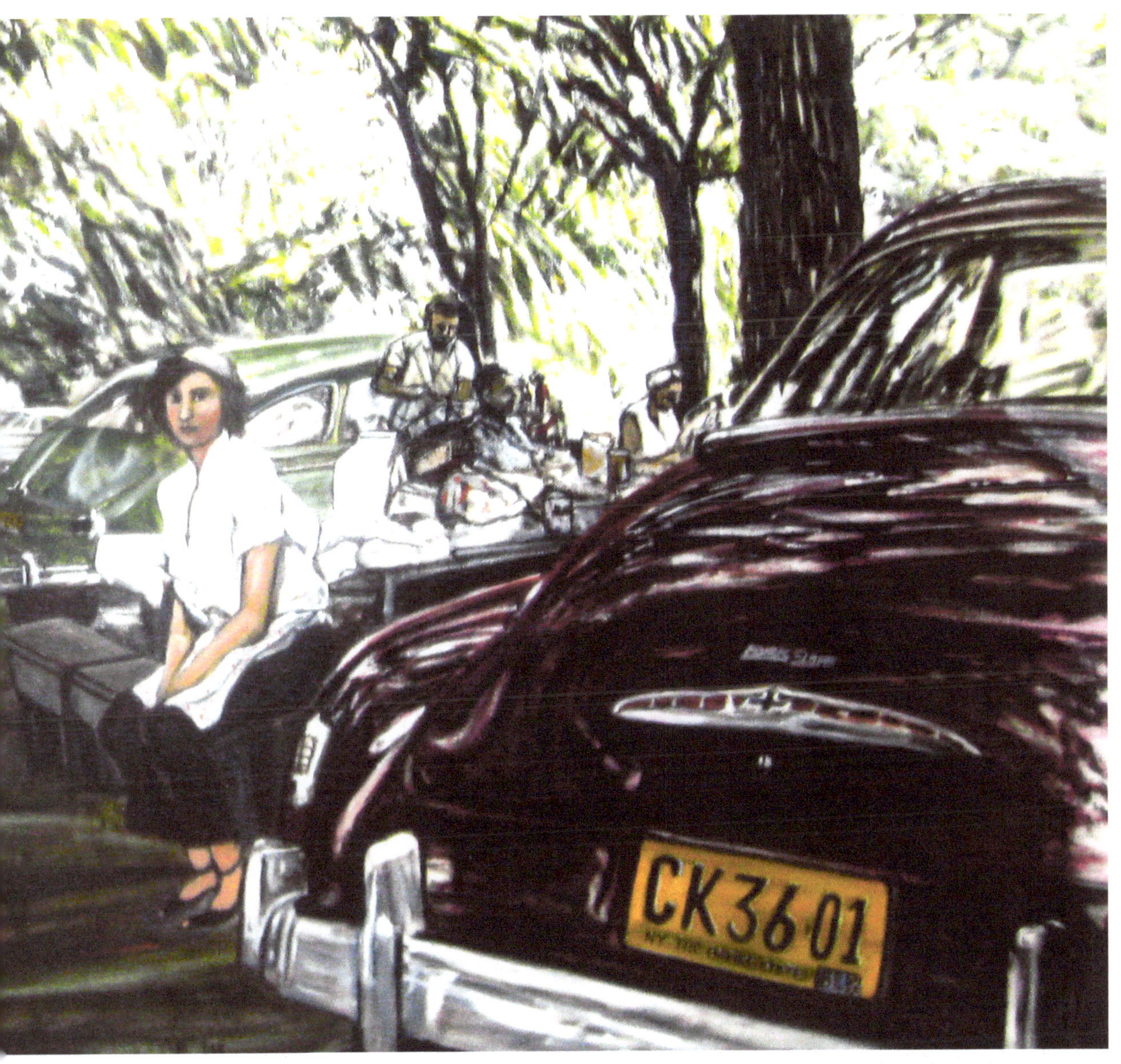

CONEY ISLAND

This painting shows my brother and me at our favorite place. I would go to Coney Island almost every day in the summer. Behind me is the parachute in Steeplechase Park and the Wonder Wheel.

The boardwalk was filled with so many wonderful people and things. The ladies playing games; the people being wheeled around. There was even a girl with an itsy-bitsy-teeny-weeny-yellow-polkadot-bikini.

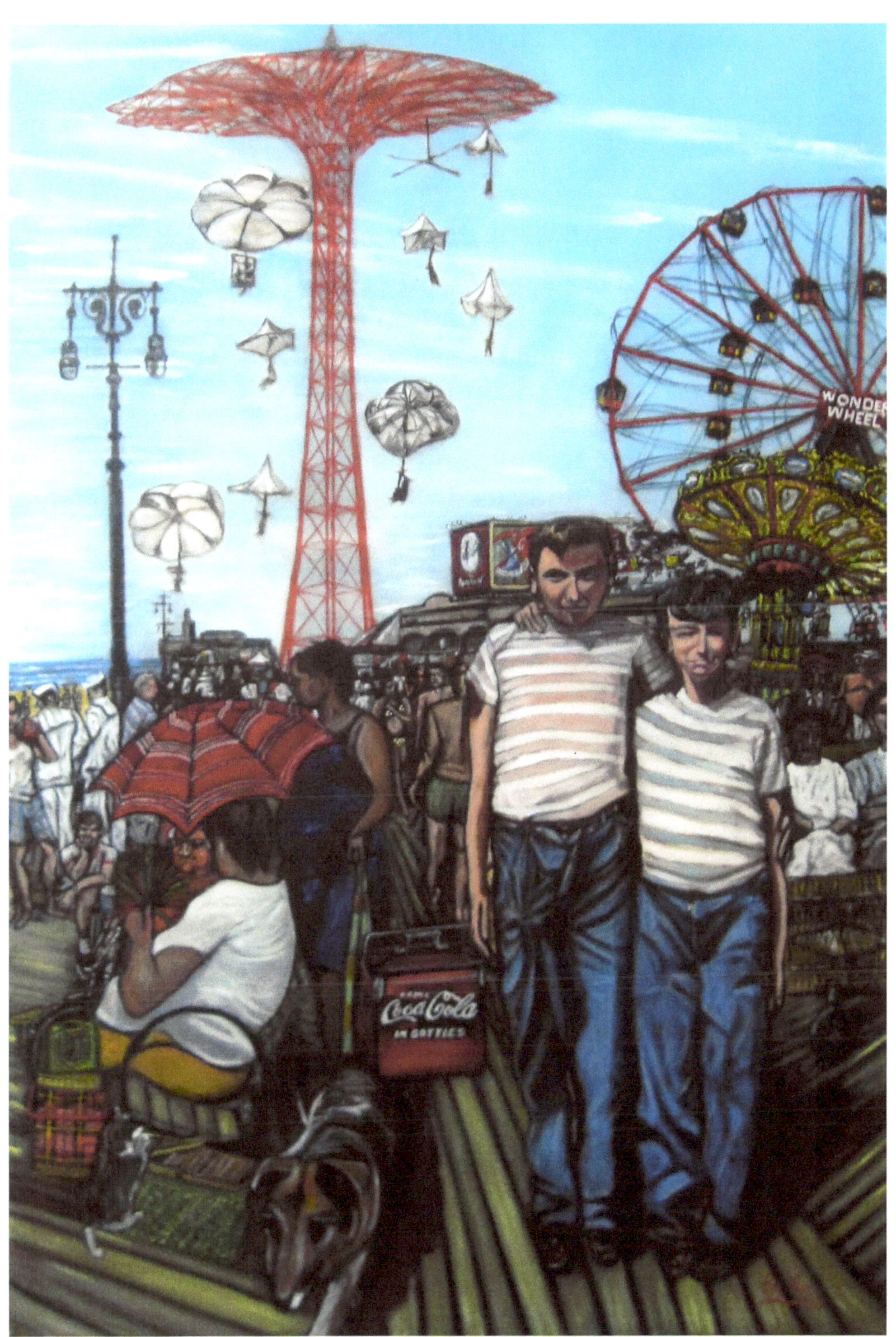
WONDER WHEEL
Coca-Cola

NATHAN'S

This is a painting of me with my father and brother in front of Nathan's, world famous for its hot dogs. I remember how popular the place was. With 25 cents in my pocket, I would go to Coney Island. It cost me 10 cents to get there and back home again. I'd use the remaining 15 cents to buy two hot dogs and a root beer soda.

When my father took my brother and me there he would treat us to hamburgers, french fries, and custard, which is what those of us from Brooklyn called soft-serve ice cream.

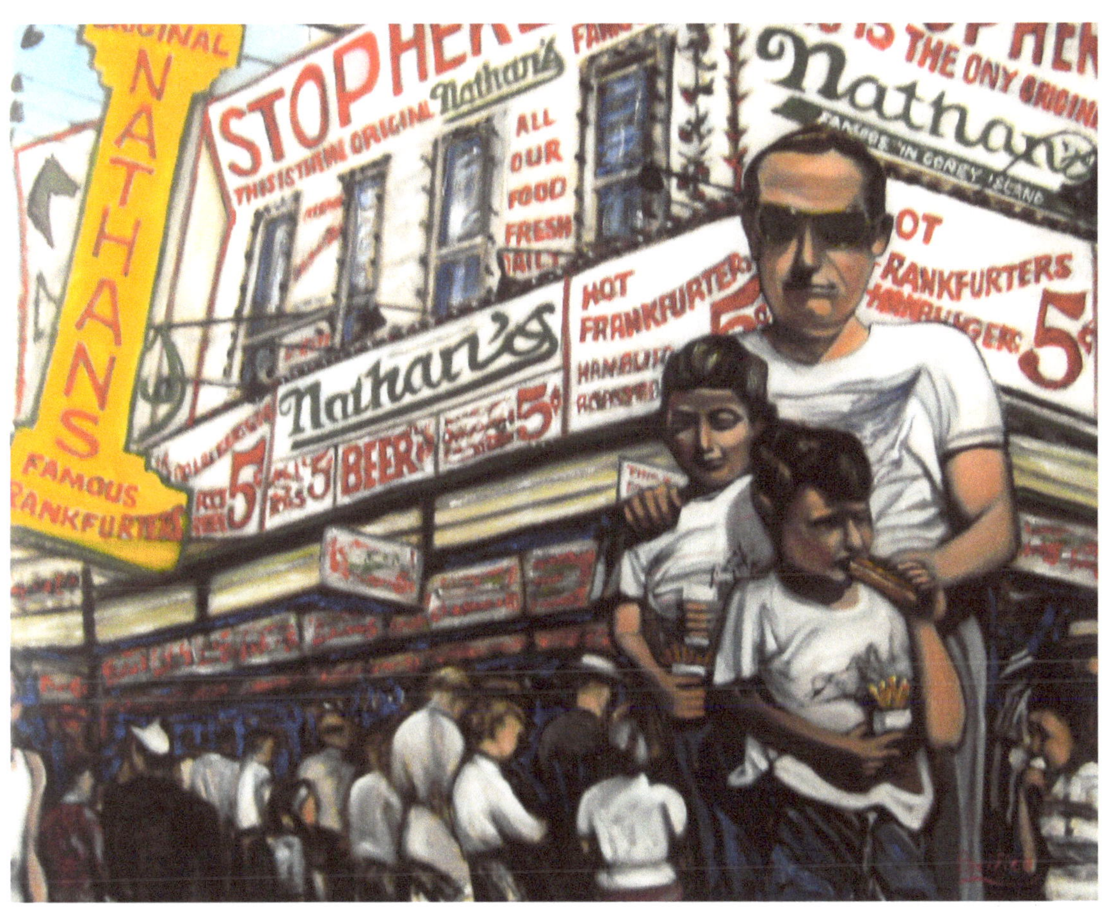

NATHAN'S
FAMOUS
STOP
Nathan's
ALL
OUR
FOOD
FRESH
HOT
FRANKFURTERS
5¢
BEER
THE ONY ORIGINAL
IN CONEY ISLAND

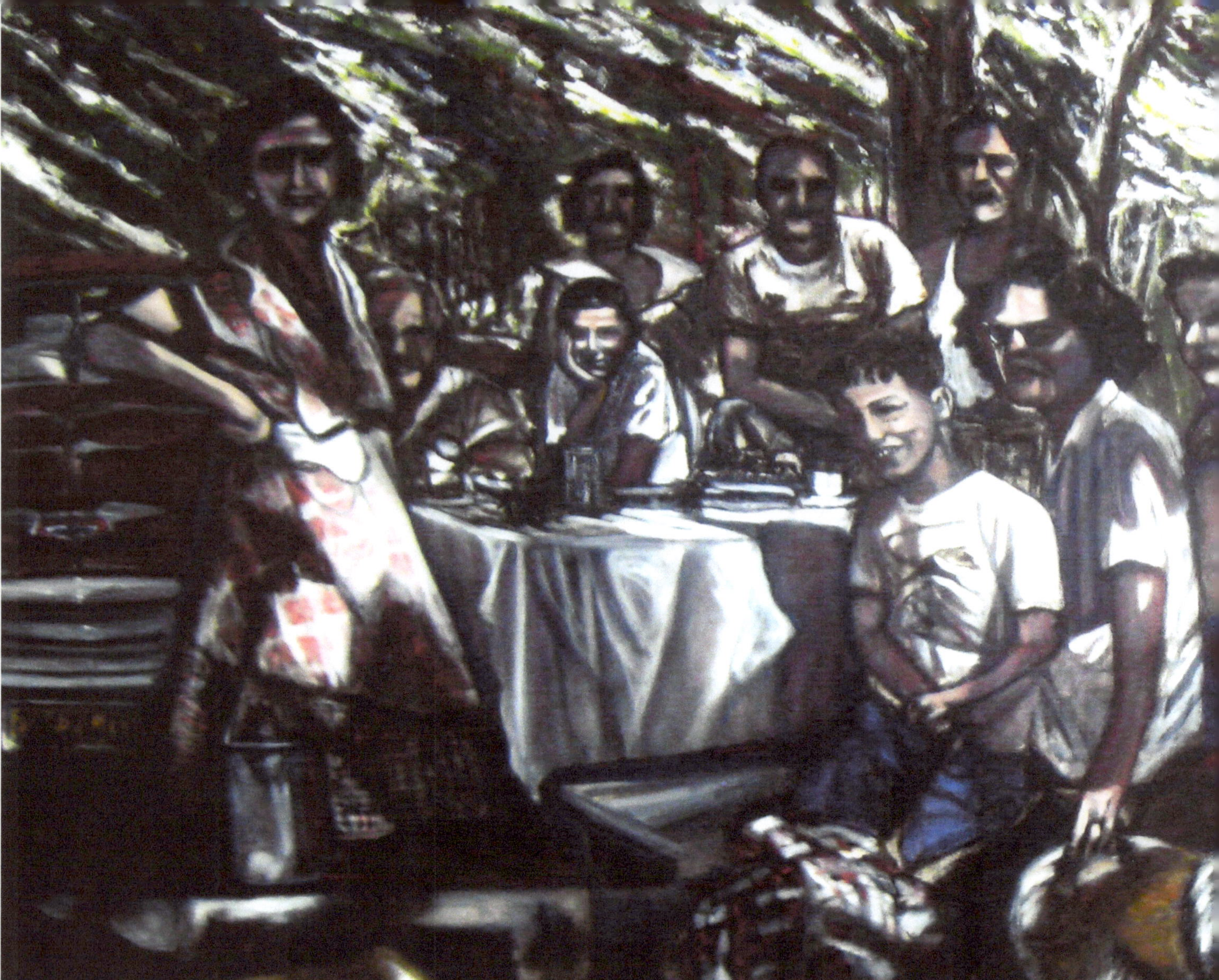

AN ITALIAN SUNDAY SUMMER PICNIC

I will never forget our Sunday summer picnics. I was so excited for them that I rarely slept the night before. We would wake up at 5 a.m. to get to the 6 a.m. Mass. After Mass, we would get ice, then pick up my mother and meet whoever was going. This painting shows my mother's girlfriends. Lucy is on the left (we called her Dodo, because she was always doing something silly) and her mother, Camella, on the right. Next to Camella are her three daughters, Martha, Gloria, and Tootsie, who was petting her dog when this picture was taken. In front of Gloria

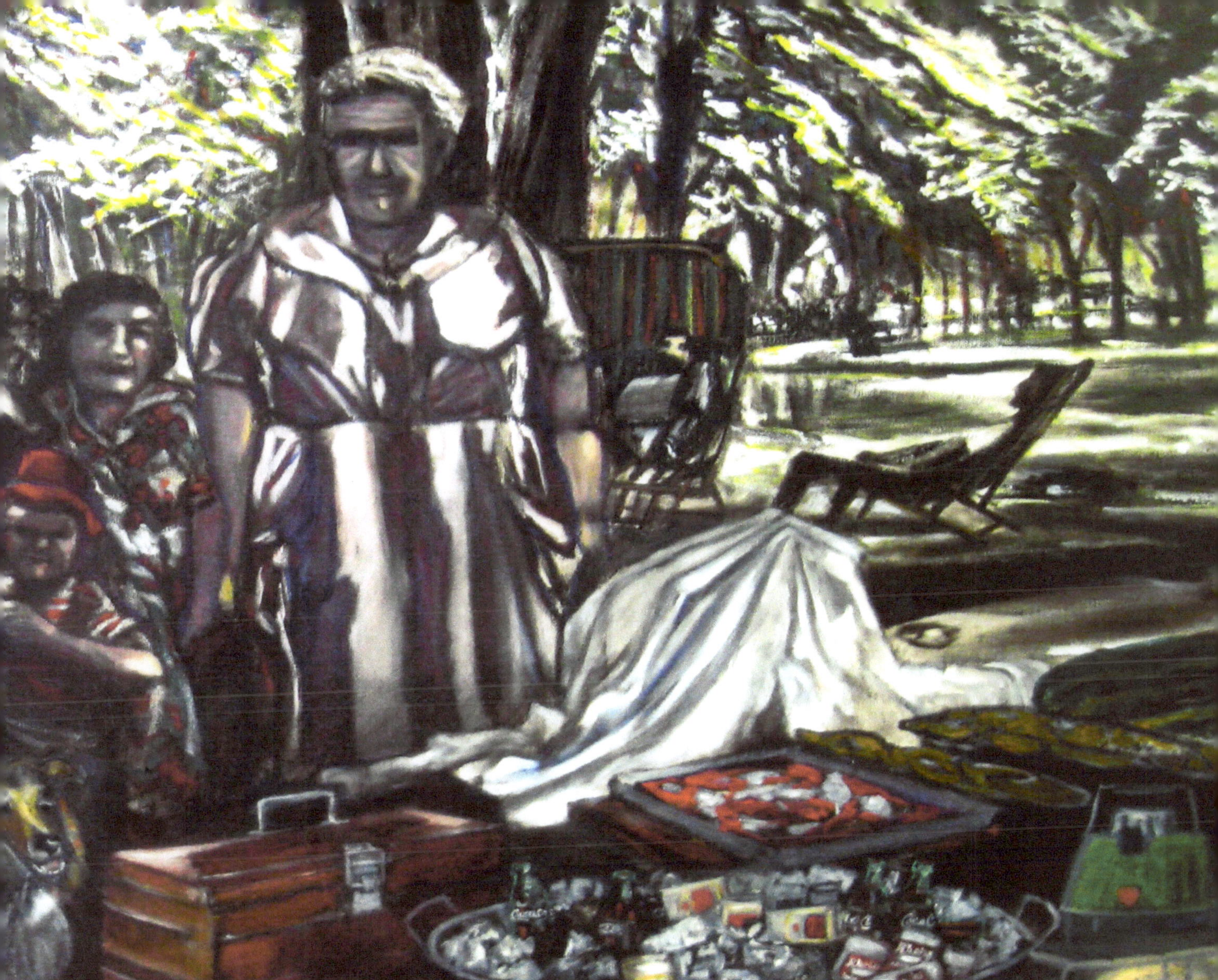

is her son Gerard. My brother Michael is next to Tootsie. In the back row is Lucy's brother Louie, my parents, and Lucy's husband, Mike. My mother would cook sauce from scratch, and we'd eat and drink all day long: wine and beer for the grown-ups and soda for us kids. I remember once saying to my mother, "Ma, I saw these people—they came into the park with a little basket. They pulled a blanket from the basket and sat down. Then they took a sandwich from the basket and began to eat it." She looked at me and said, "They don't know how to eat."

AUNT HELEN AT 60

This is my Great Aunt Helen on her 60th birthday. She was my grandmother's sister. She lived upstairs, in my parents' house in Brooklyn. The picture this portrait is based on was taken in her apartment on April 1, sometime in the early 1960s. Helen was an Aries like me. I said, "Aunt Helen, it's your birthday. I want to take your picture." She said, "Ok. Let's have some fun."

She disappeared into her closet and came out wearing a green bridesmaid's gown (whose it was, I'll never know). Then she proceeded to take all the bows from the presents that we had given her and put them in her hair. After that, she sat in her chair and smiled at me. But before I could take the picture, she cried, "Wait!" She picked up the artificial flowers from the coffee table next to her, then she smiled at me once more and said, "How do I look?" I replied, "Great!" Then I snapped the picture. It became *Aunt Helen at 60.*

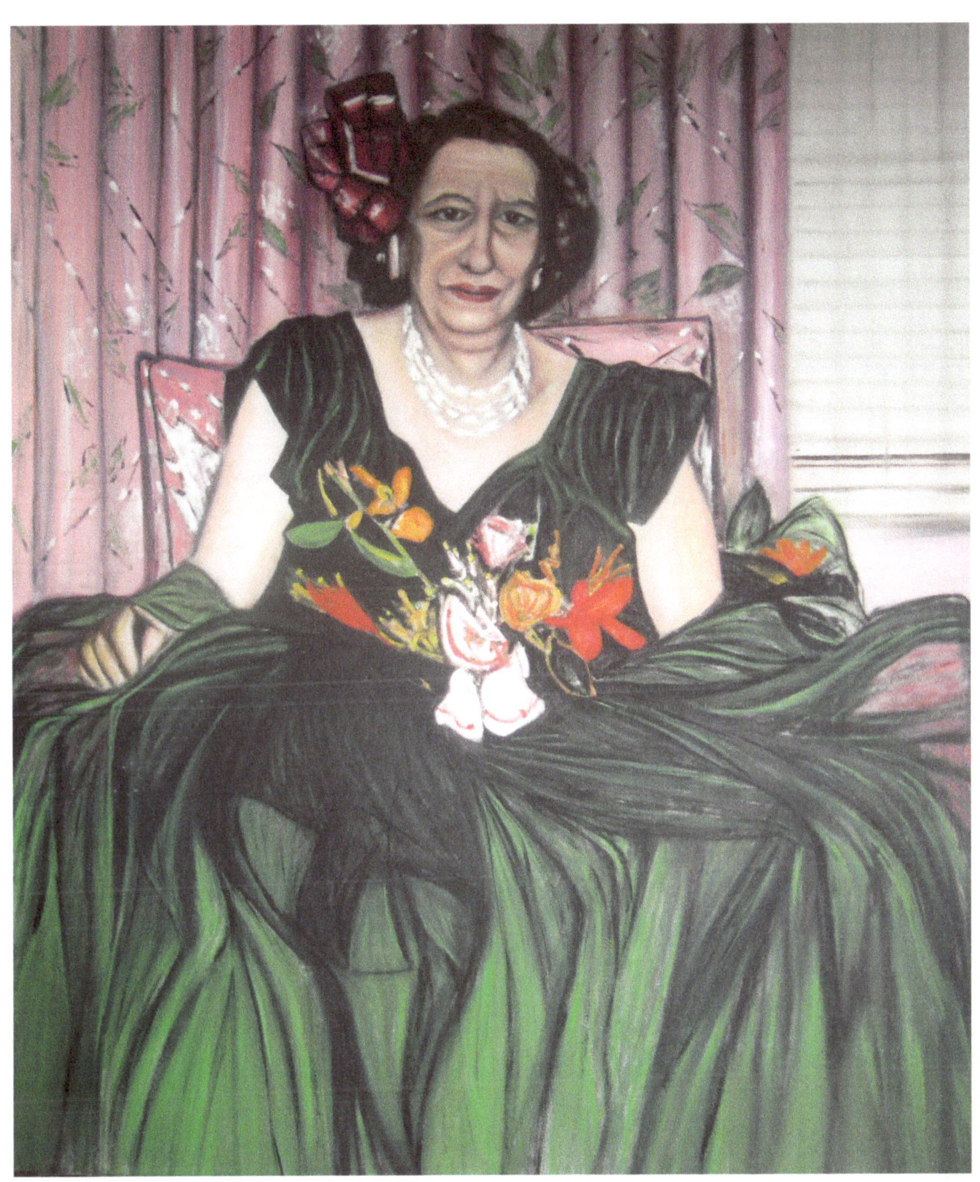

"AWAY WE GO"

One hot summer afternoon, my family decided to make a shower in our garden by taking the hose and tying it to the clothesline. We changed into our bathing suits and turned it on. Aunt Helen put on a suit too and, being the joker she was, put my father's fishing cap on her head. She then picked up a Pan Am flight bag, turned to me as I was taking her picture, and said, "Away we go."

Apparently, she had heard the phrase on the "Jackie Gleason Show" the night before. She was a hoot!

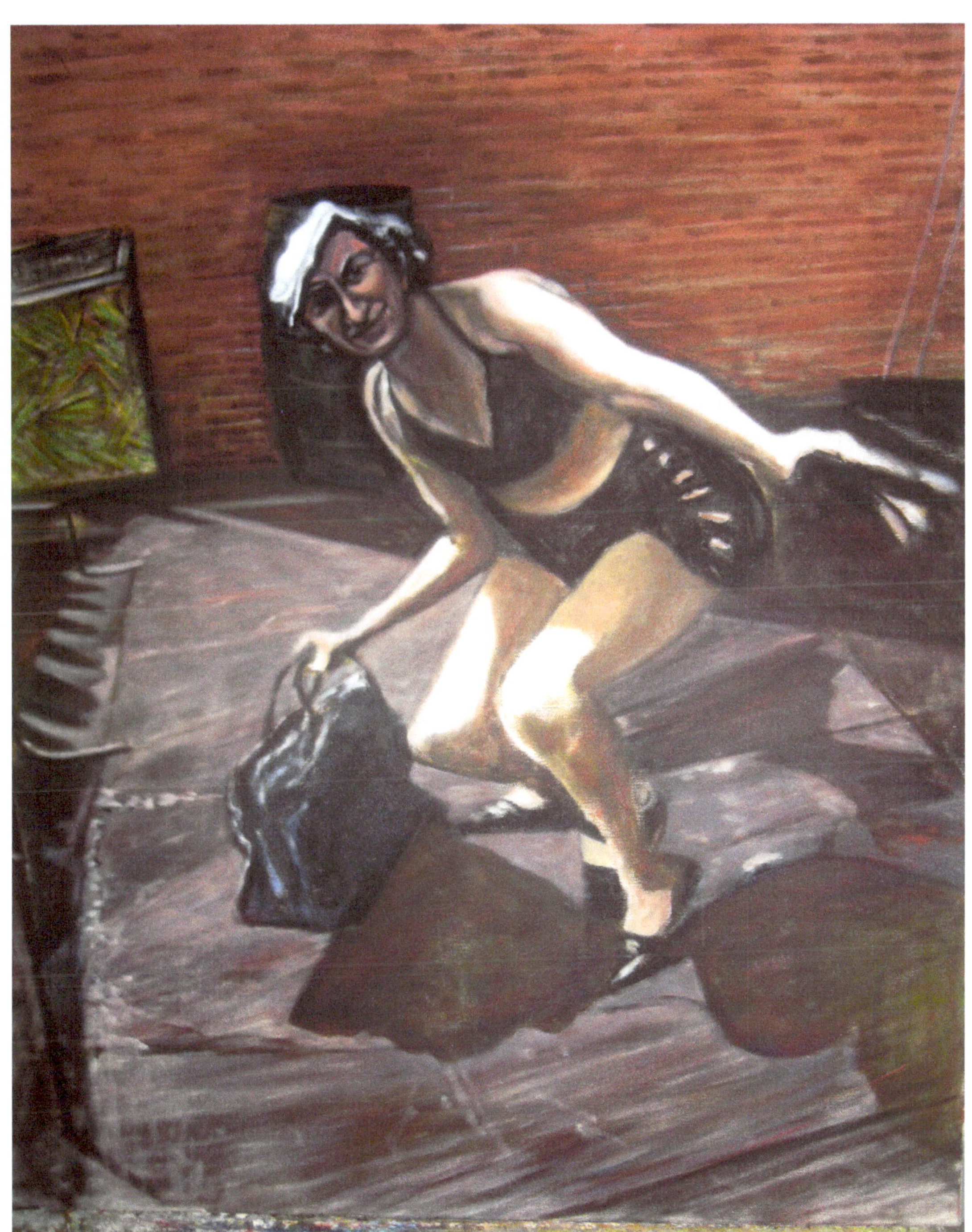

FEAST OF SAINT ANTHONY

On June 13 of every year, our church, Our Lady of Peace, would celebrate St. Anthony's Feast Day. His statue would be brought out and a lively procession would take place through the streets.

The statue would be festooned with colorful ribbons, to which people would pin dollar bills in praise of St. Anthony. A band would play Italian music as the procession continued through the neighborhood. By the time the statue made its way back to the church, it would be covered in so much money that you could barely see it. The feast would continue into the night and for the next several days. It was a combination of great food, good music, and lots of fun.

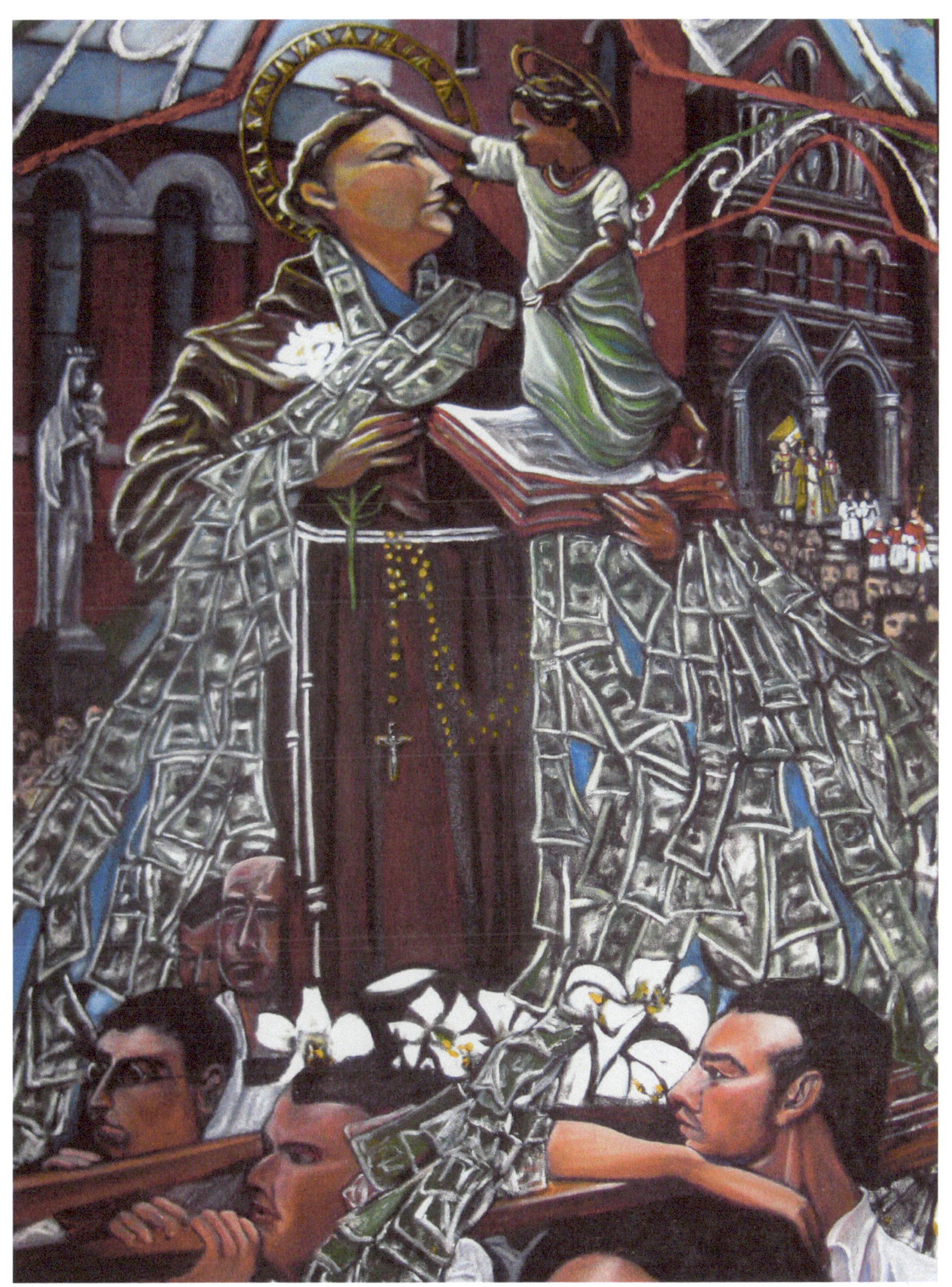

AUNT MARY'S WEDDING

This is my Aunt Mary on her wedding day in my grandmother's living room. She was a beautiful bride. Her new husband was a Polish man named Henry. Her maid of honor was her best friend Celia. Aunt Lola is in the background, and my Uncle Freddie is smoking a cigarette in the upper corner of the painting.

Aunt Mary didn't have much luck in life. Her marriage didn't last. Henry (or Hank, as we knew him) cheated on her. The only good thing that came from their marriage was their fantastic son, my cousin Chester. I loved visiting my aunt and walking Chester in his carriage.

I remember Mary always wanted to feed me, fearing that I didn't eat enough. She bought salami and Italian bread and made me sandwiches, so I would go home feeling stuffed. My mother would say, "Aren't you hungry?" And I would say, "No, you know what it's like going to Aunt Mary's. I'm going next week to help her walk Chester."

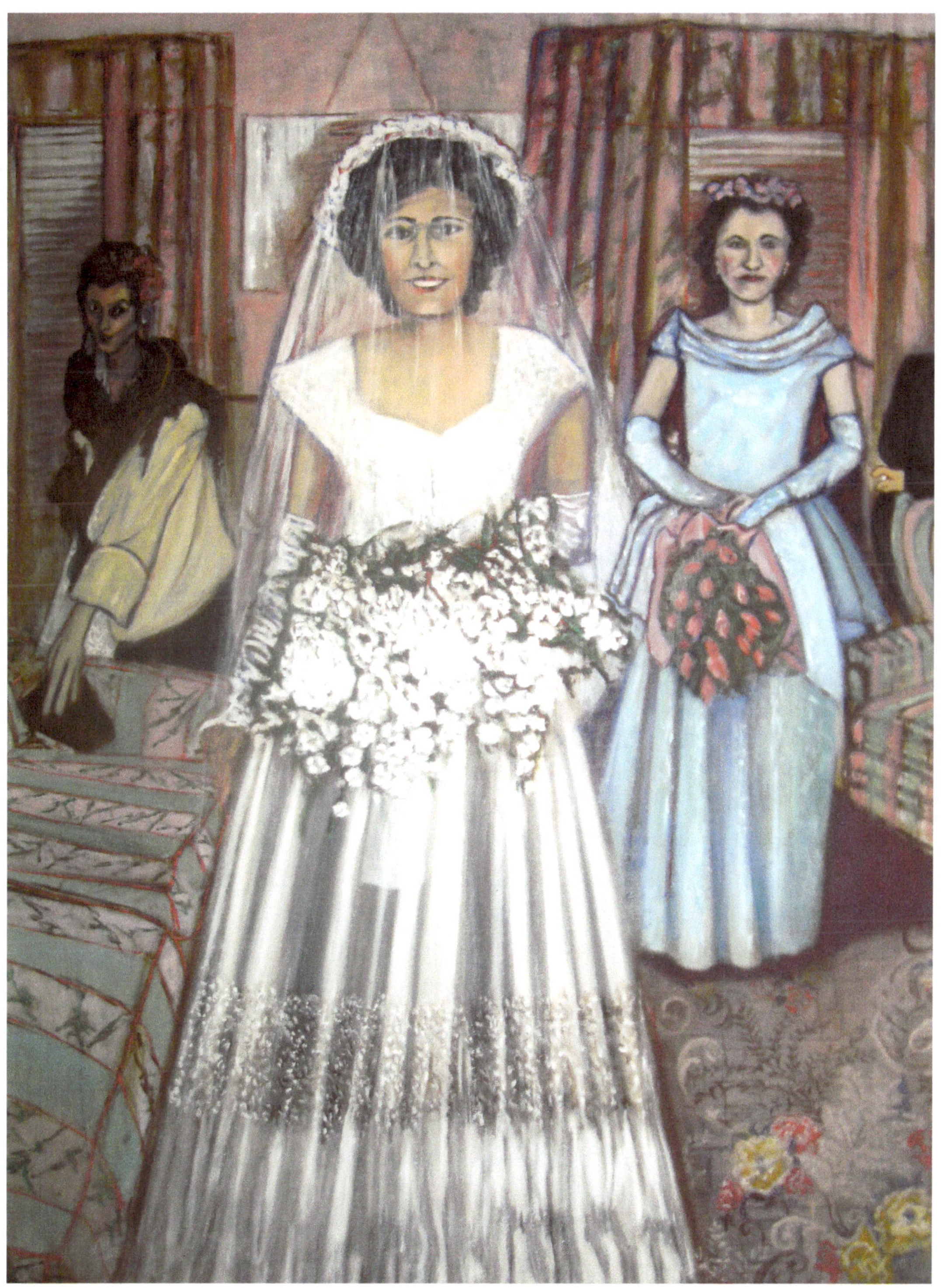

AUNT MARY, COUSIN CHESTER

Aunt Mary, my mother's sister, and her husband, Henry Kubinski, a Polish man, had a son, my cousin Chester. Later in life, Chester decided to change his name to David Evens, because he didn't want to have a Polish-sounding name.

When Michael and I had our neon gallery in the Village we would often see Chester walking with a friend. One evening, he introduced us to him. His name was Howard Ashman and he told us they had just had dinner with Peggy Lee. We thought he was a little off, but it was true. Howard, it turns out, was a very successful songwriter. He wrote lyrics for *Little Shop of Horrors, The Little Mermaid*, and *Beauty and the Beast*.

Chester (or David) moved to Chicago after having an argument with Howard. Three months later, he came back. He wasn't feeling well. Three months after that, he died of AIDS.

My Aunt Mary was in the hospital herself with cancer. It was the most difficult day of my life when Aunt Lola and I had to go to the hospital to tell her that Chester was dead. My aunt came to the funeral parlor and just stared at her son, never saying a word.

Being Jewish, Howard couldn't understand a Christian wake at all. He was so depressed. Then a month after Chester's death, Aunt Mary died. Howard died a year later. When he won an Academy Award for *Little Mermaid,* we watched on the television as his sister accepted the Oscar for him. What did they all do to deserve this?

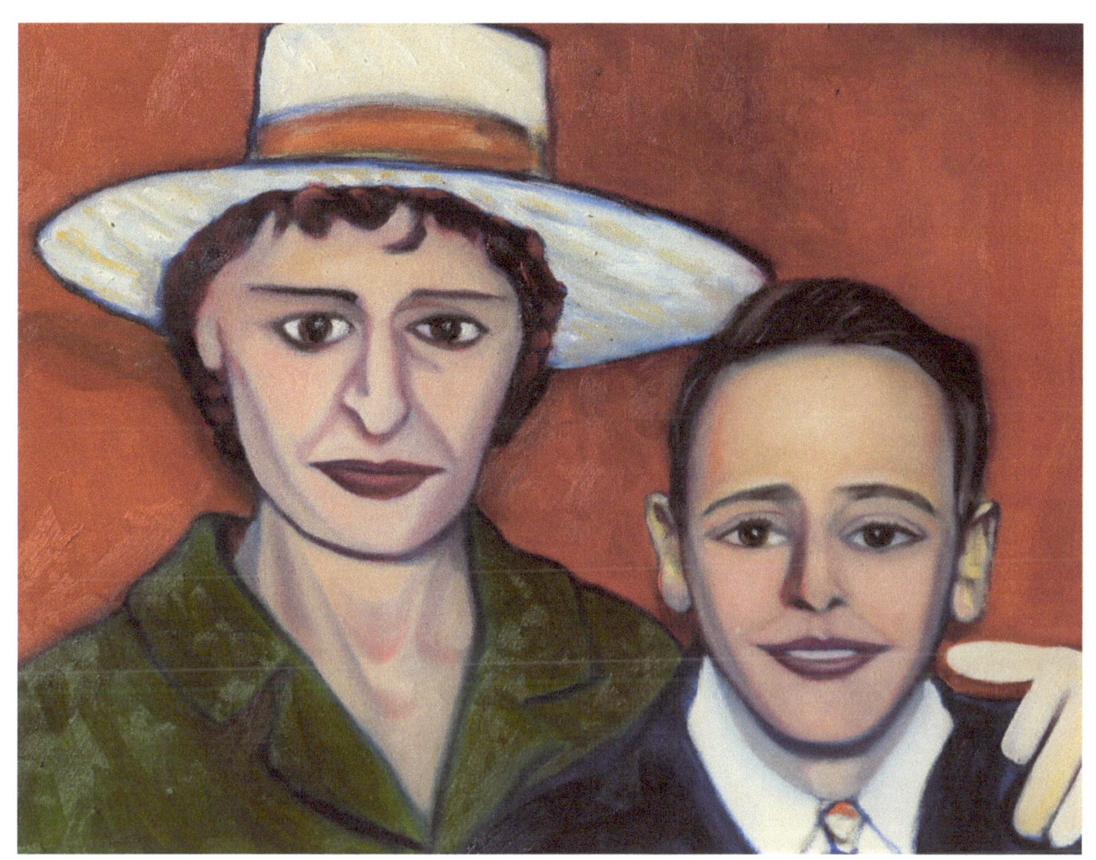

UNDER THE BOARDWALK

I loved going to Coney Island. I would get on the subway and take it to Stillwell Avenue, the last stop to Coney Island. My father would take us there a lot, but my mother didn't like sitting on the hot sand and in the hot sun, so she didn't go too often. The one time she took my brother and me, she convinced her best friend to join us. Her name was Lucy, but everybody called her DoDo, because she was always doing something: shopping, cleaning, cooking. She never stopped moving. Like my mother, she refused to sit in the sun, so the perfect place for her and my mother was under the boardwalk. I never understood why they liked it there. To me, it was strange to go to the beach and stay under the boardwalk, where it was damp and cold and smelly.

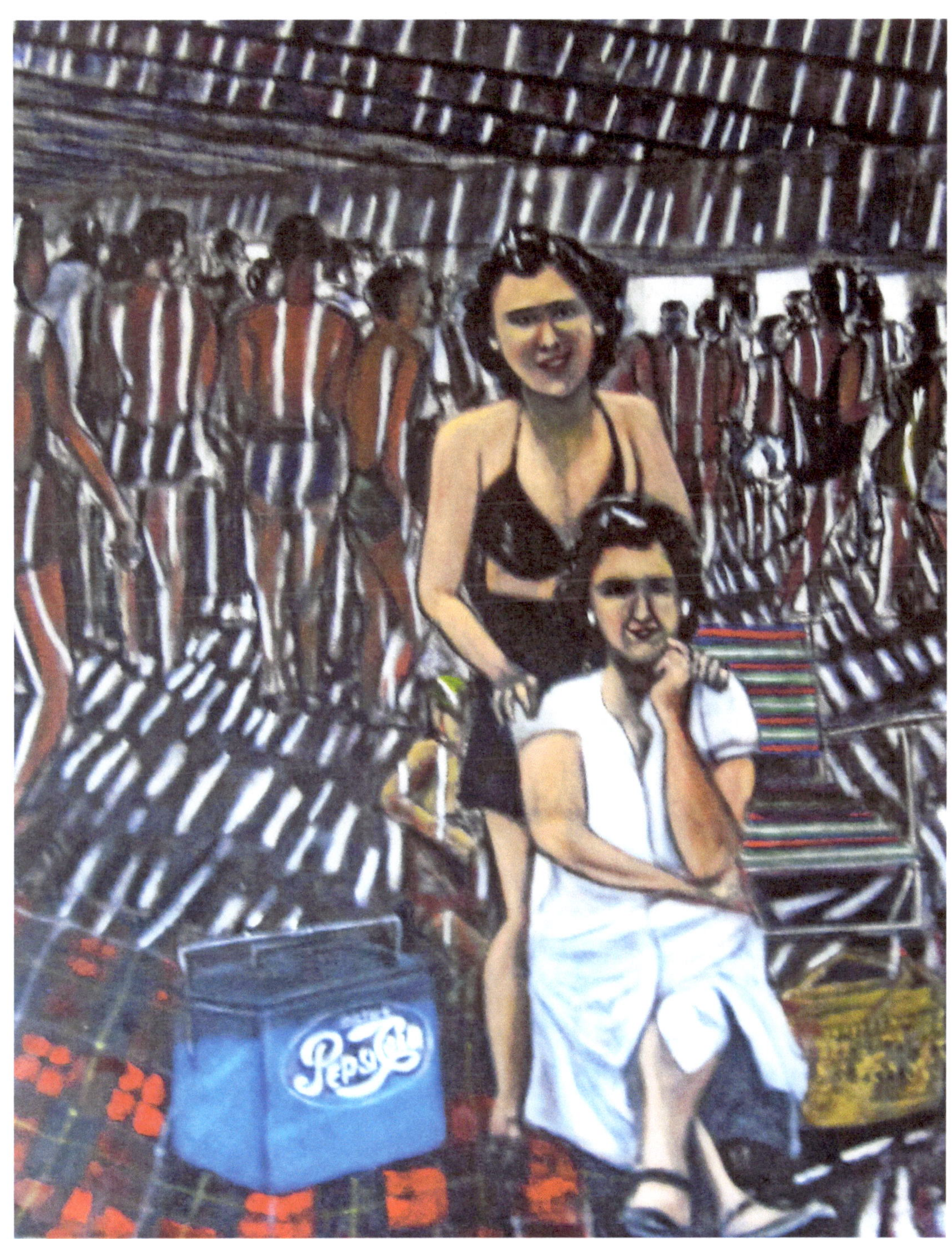

AUNT LOLA AT 50

This is my Aunt Lola, at the age of 50. Doesn't she look great holding that cigarette. Check out that come-hither smile. You wouldn't think it, but she was a rather shy person. She had a big heart and was very kind. She was always well dressed, and looked beautiful all the time.

She had a certain air and style about her. When she walked down the street, heads would turn. She'll always be my favorite aunt. I thought she should have been a model. In fact, when I was in the advertising business, I cast her in a few of my ads. As the saying goes, "Whatever Lola wants, Lola gets."

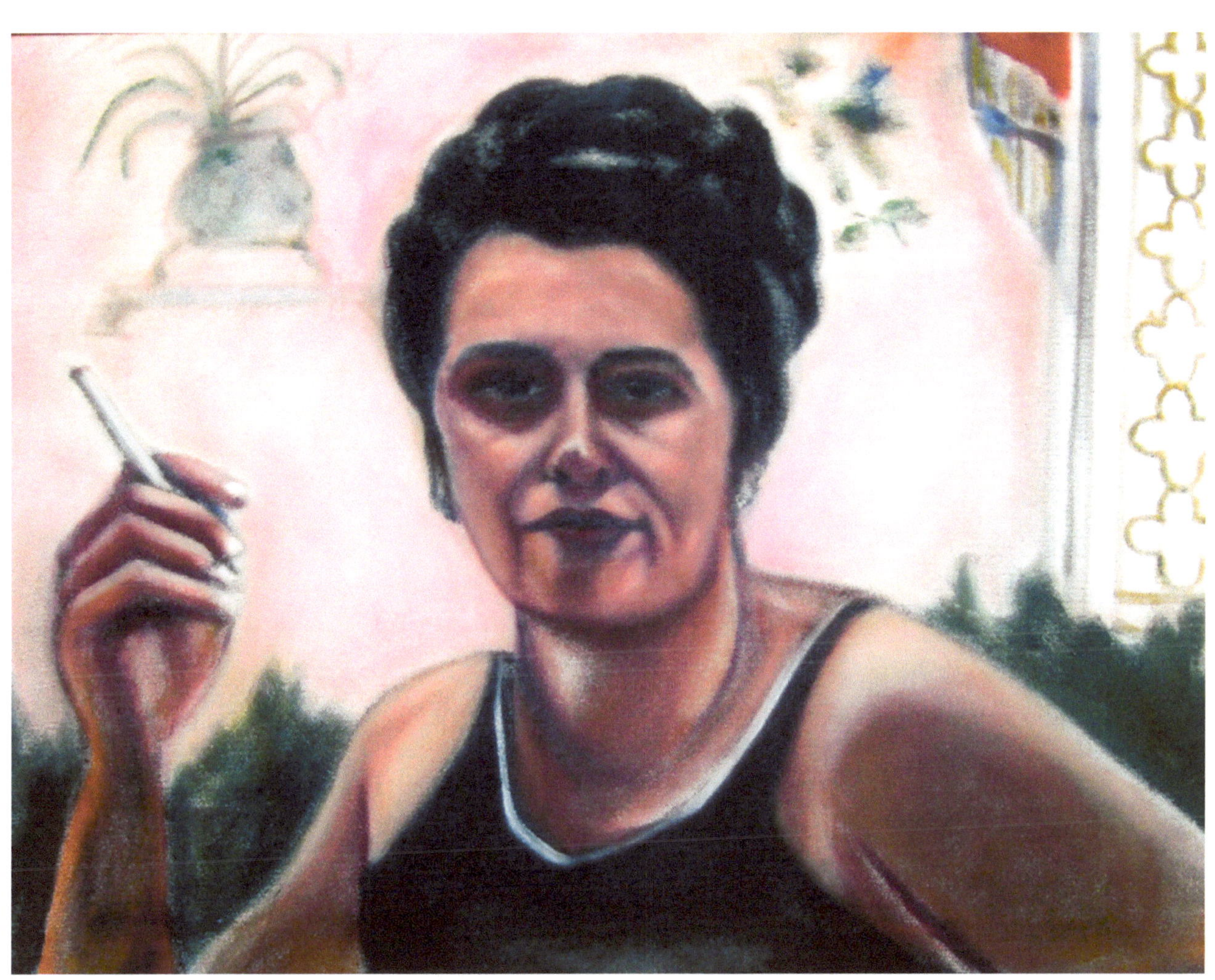

AUNT JULIA

Aunt Julia was my father's sister. Besides Julia, there was Madelin, Beatrice, Rosie, Anna, Julia and Louisa. My father, Anthony, was the only boy. Almost every day I would play with my twin cousins, Pargie and Vincent. They lived down the block from me. Aunt Julia was their mother. They lived above my Uncle Tony's barber shop. I would walk down the block and holler under their window until Aunt Julia or one of the twins would say, "Come on up."

They lived on the top floor. She would let me into the apartment. There would be my cousin Anthony studying, Joey was with his girlfriend Tina. Aunt Julia was cooking for the family. We would go to our Aunt Beatrice's to meet up with our cousin, Angela. Those were the days. We could always find something interesting to do. We loved going to New York to dance on the TV show, *Teen Bandstand*, at least once a week.

In the summer, we would take the train to Coney Island. We hung out on Bay 13, which was close to the Stillwell Avenue train station and to Nathan's.

Years later, Aunt Julia and Uncle Tony moved into my parents' house. I remember her leaning out the window waiting for the "chicken man," who would drive by in a truck selling fresh chickens. I would say "hi, Aunt Julia" as I looked up to greet her.

I photographed her one summer when she came to visit us in Colrain. I always loved that photograph that I took of her. My cousin Jonathan, who is the son of my Cousin Anthony, came to visit a few years later. He also liked the photo and commissioned me to paint a portrait of her.

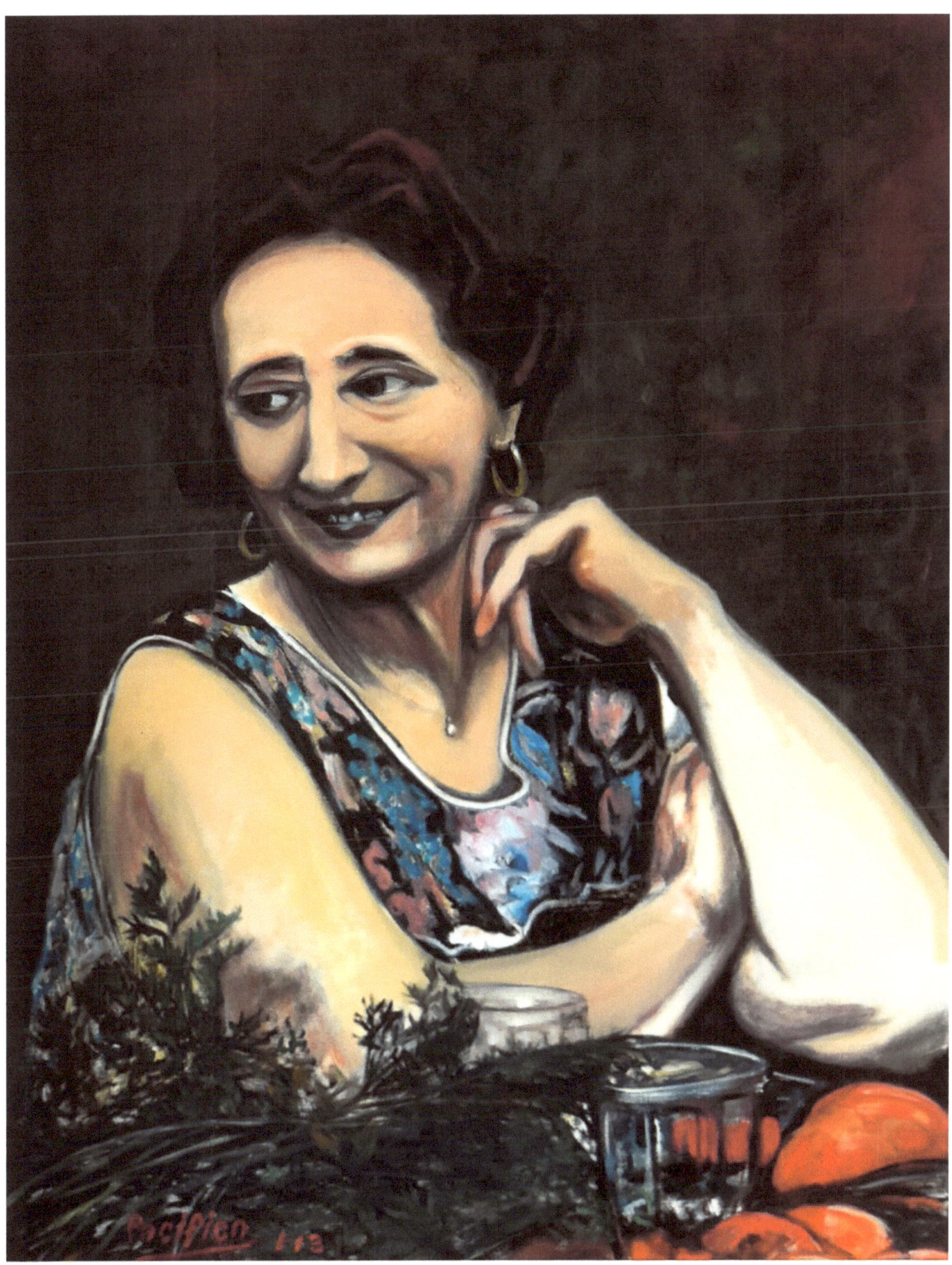

AUNT JULIA'S AND UNCLE TONY'S 50TH WEDDING ANNIVERSARY

My cousin Jonathan commissioned me to paint a second painting, this time of Aunt Julia and Uncle Tony. He showed me a photograph he had of their 50th wedding anniversary.

I remember the event so well, it was great. I had given them a neon sign I created for them. Aunt Julia looked beautiful and Uncle Tony was so proud. Cousin Jonathan is my second cousin. He has a fabulous business, Raiola Company, that creates fantastic events.

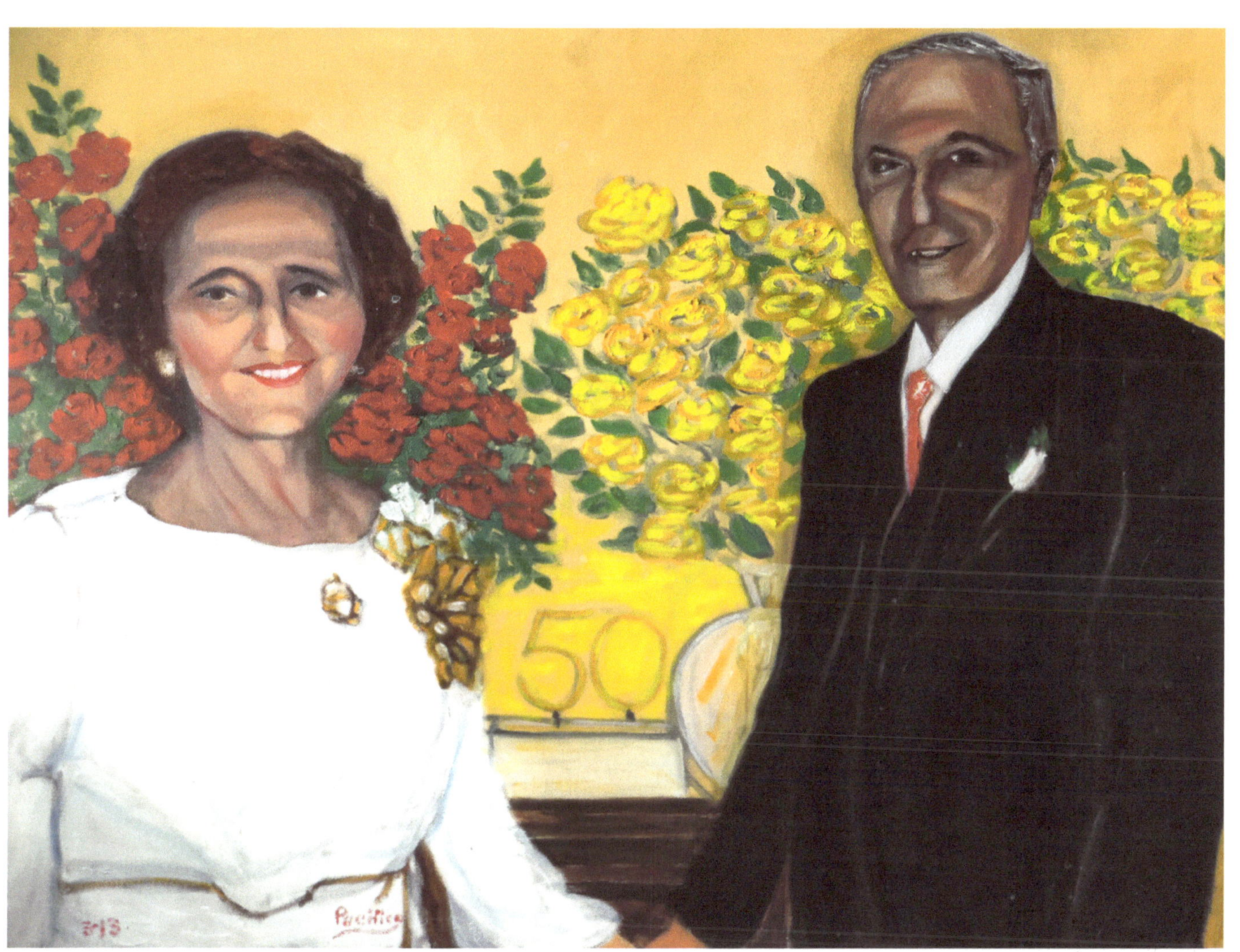
50

A YOUNGER ME

At my age, it is hard for me to remember exactly what I was like as a child. I was kind of shy, very proper. I wore a suit and tie a lot. I thought that was what you were supposed to do.

I don't remember who took the photo this painting is based on, but I know it was taken in my parents' living room, probably on a Sunday. That was the day when I dressed up the most. The truth is, I probably couldn't wait to put on something more comfortable and go down to the basement to paint.

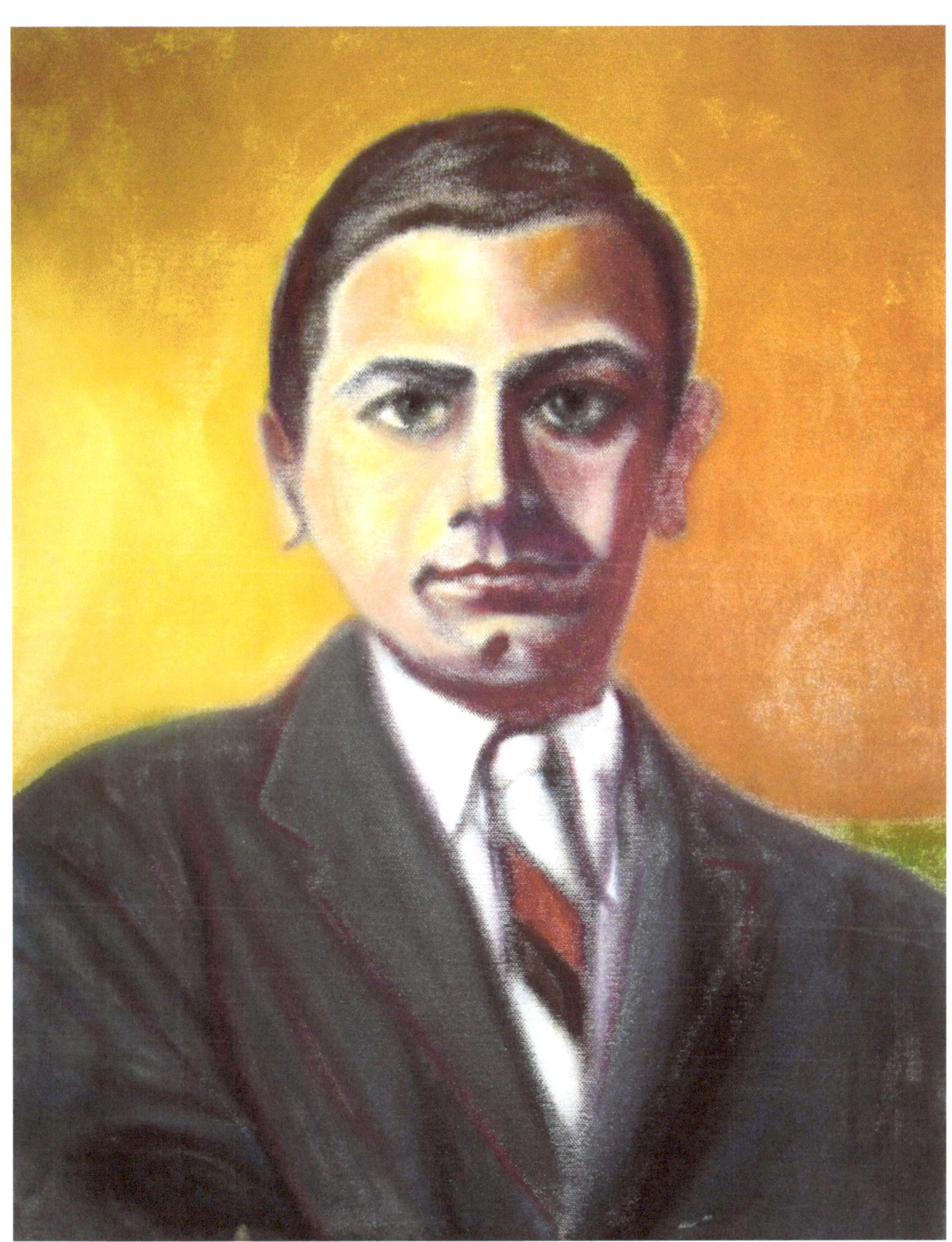

AUNT TESSIE

Aunt Tessie was my mother's youngest sister. She always babysat my brother and me.

My most vivid memory is of her coming home from work, climbing up the stairs to my grandmother's apartment singing her favorite song, "Besame Mucho."

I had a difficult time figuring out how to paint her. I loved her very much. She would take me to Coney Island when she was on vacation. She became ill with rheumatoid arthritis when she was in her late 20s. After that, she was always in pain.

One Easter, as my aunts were admiring my cousin Susan's Easter hat and passing it around to one another, they placed it on Aunt Tessie's head. She smiled and I snapped the picture. I tried to capture the pain that she was suffering. You can see the pain in her body. Her hands were contorted, and it was even difficult for her to smile.

She died in her early 40s, after being in the hospital for about two years.

To me she will always be Saint Theresa.

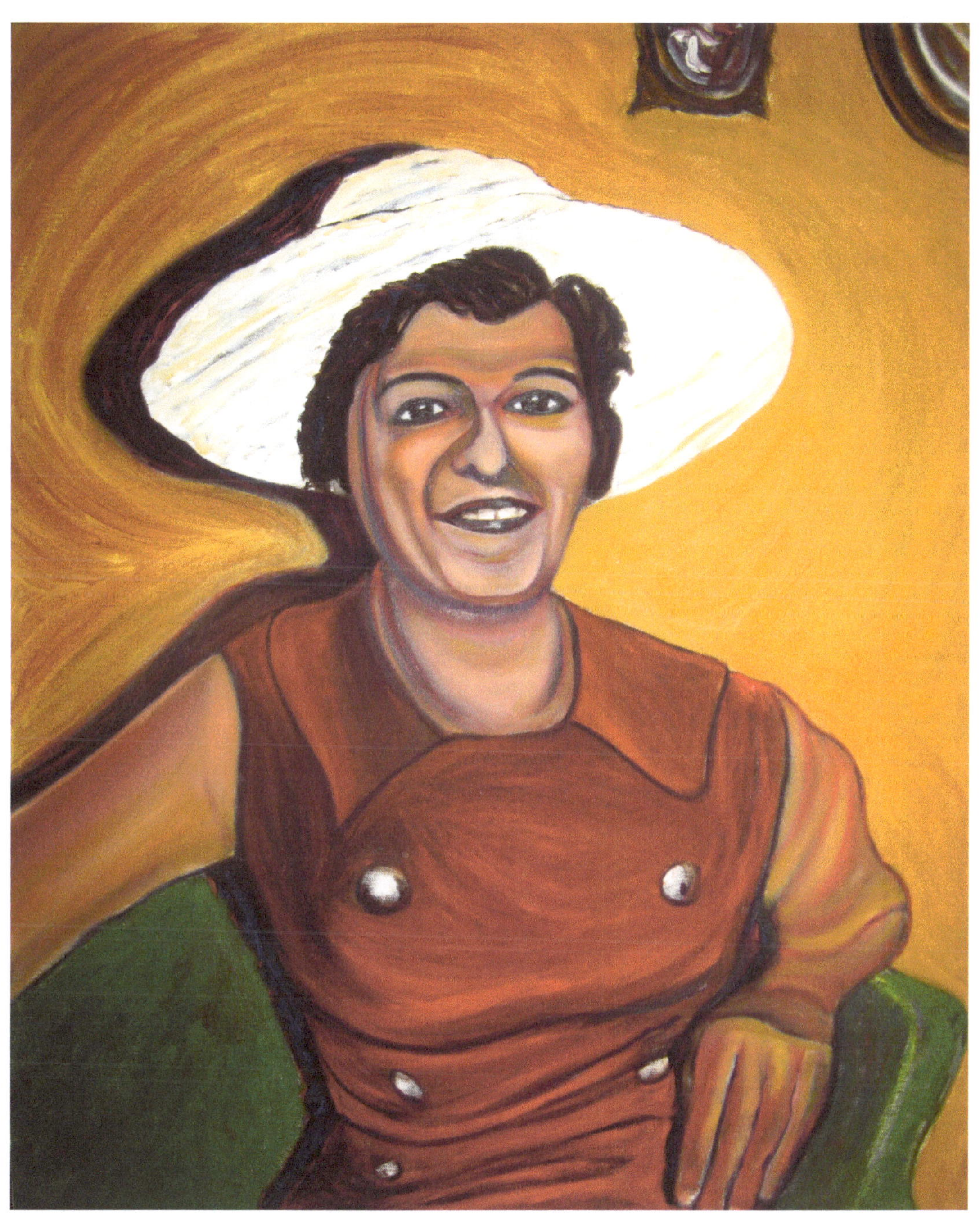

MAMA MIA MAKING LASAGNA

One Sunday morning, I walked into my mother's kitchen and found her making lasagna. I grabbed my camera and said, "Ma, look at me." She turned and smiled as I took her picture. She was wearing a colorful MuMu. It was a popular apron that a lot of Italian housewives wore in those days.

On this day, my mother was unraveling a strand of lasagna pasta and placing it into the baking dish on the table. You can see the ricotta cheese in front of her and the sauce for the lasagna in the pot on her Maytag stove. Her colander had only one handle, but she never parted with it. She loved to cook. It was the joy of her life—and mine, too.

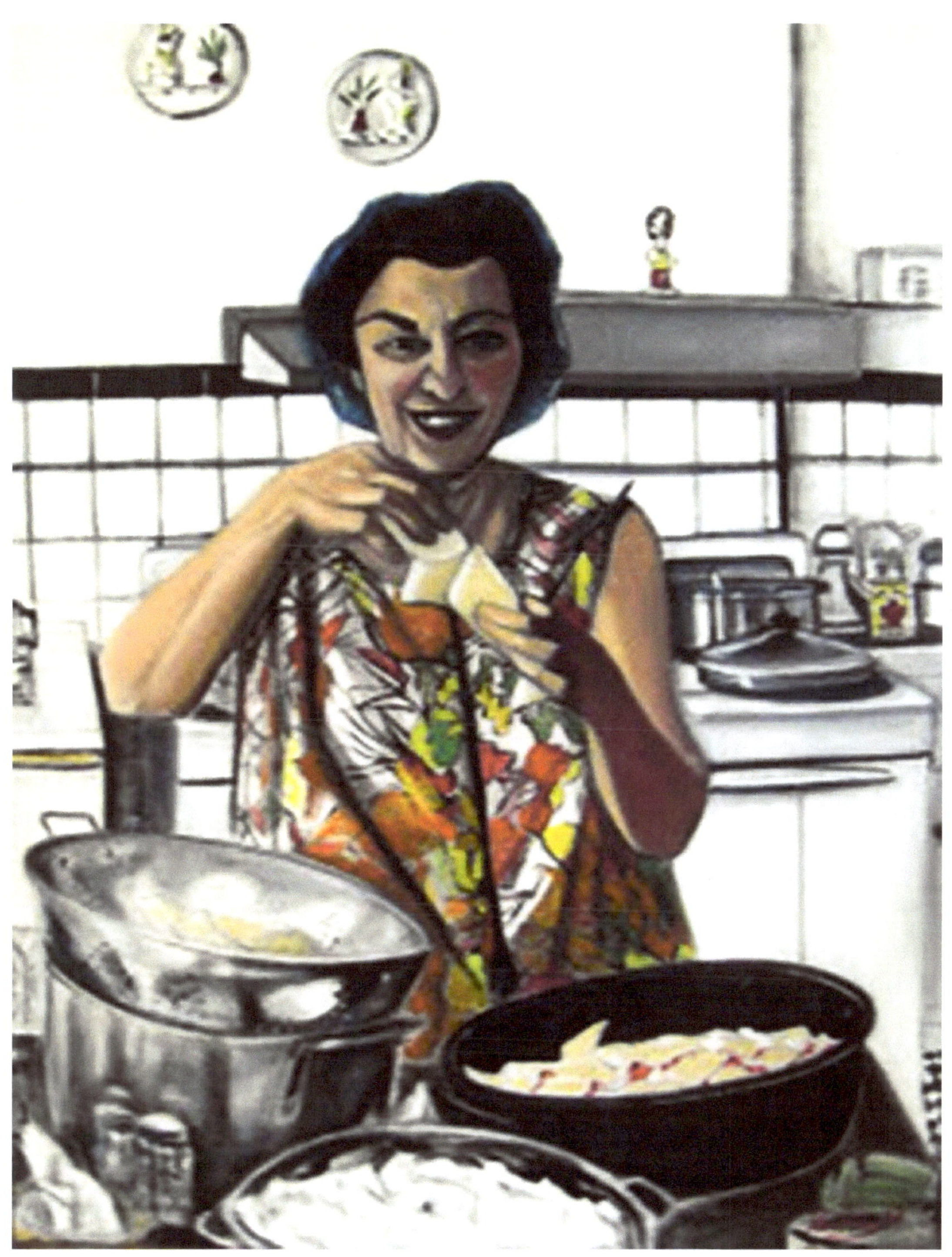

GOUMADA

When I was in the Army, I was assigned to the Signal Core at the Army Pictorial Center in Long Island City. One of our assignments was to cover the World's Fair in Flushing Meadows, New York. While there, I visited the Japanese pavilion and saw the Nikon camera display. My eyes immediately went to the new Nikon F. The man behind the counter told me that they were going to go on sale after the fair was over because they didn't want to take the cameras back to Japan, so I came back another day and bought the new Nikon F. for about $300.

One Sunday morning as I was enjoying my new toy, I visited my parents' house in Brooklyn. I had a roll of black-and-white film in the camera at the time. As I strolled into their garden. I saw my Uncle Philly talking to my neighbor Jennie. He was in his typical manly position, looking so proud and macho up against the fence. Jennie, her hair in curlers, had a wide smile on her face. She seemed to be in some sort of euphoric state. She was so close to Uncle Philly that if she leaned against the fence any harder, she would have fallen face first into my parents' garden.

I thought nothing of them being in this position at the time, and they barely noticed my presence. The lighting on them was so strong and the garden behind Jennie, resplendent with its grape vines and roses, seemed so beautiful that I had to capture the moment with my new camera. I snapped a picture of them and continued on my way, taking more pictures in the garden.

About five years ago, as I was contemplating *My Italian Story,* I showed my album of photos to my cousin Susan, my Uncle Philly

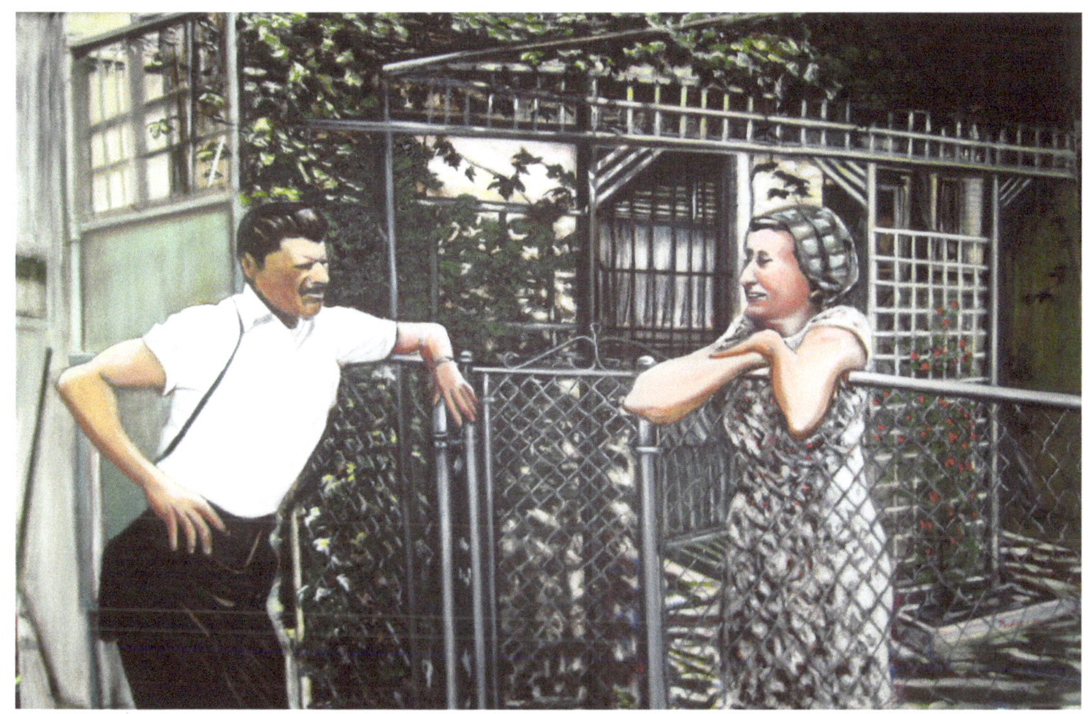

and Aunt Lola's daughter. As soon as she saw the picture of her father talking to Jennie, she screamed to me: "That's her! That's her! She's the SOB that my father cheated on my mother with!"

So, I give you "Goumada," southern Italian slang for "mistress."

AUNT LOLA UNDER THE FIG TREE

Aunt Lola was my favorite of my mother's sisters, even though I loved them all. I took the photo for this painting. I thought the outfit that she was wearing looked great on her. For this picture, I took her into my parents' garden and placed her in front of their fig tree. She had on these white gloves that only she could wear. She looked so very Italian.

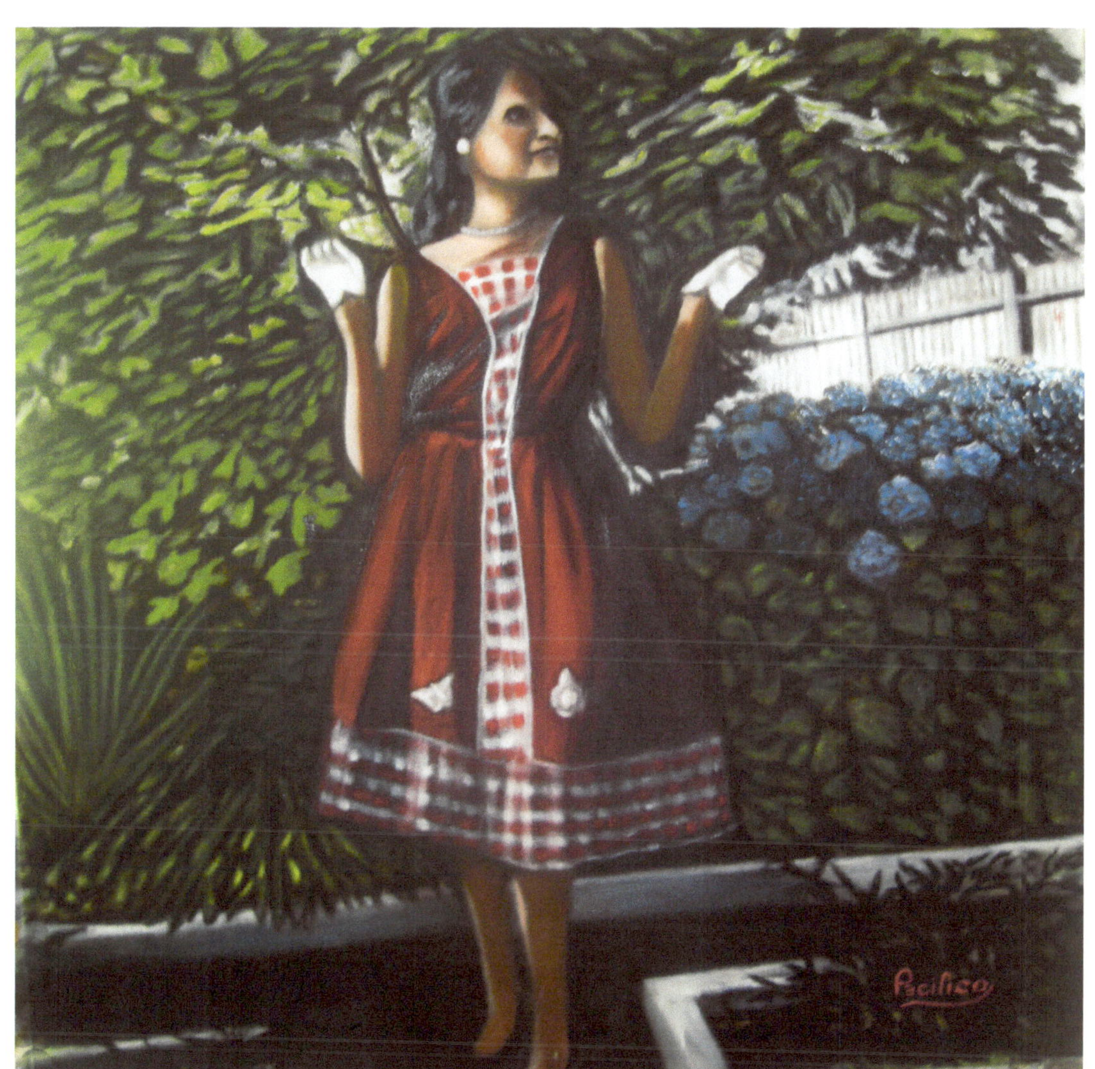

THE GYPSY

Every time I went to Coney Island by train, I would pass the gypsy. She was enclosed in a metal box near the Wonder Wheel. She was old and scary, dressed in white with a lace shawl over her shoulders. She had pearls around her neck and tarot cards fanned out under her hands.

I loved finding out what she had to say. I would put a dime in the slot and she would move her head as if to look at me and smile. Her hands would seemingly float back and forth over the cards and then, suddenly, my fortune would come out of a slot. I would hope her message was a good one. I smiled back at her almost all the time because she usually had good things to say to me.

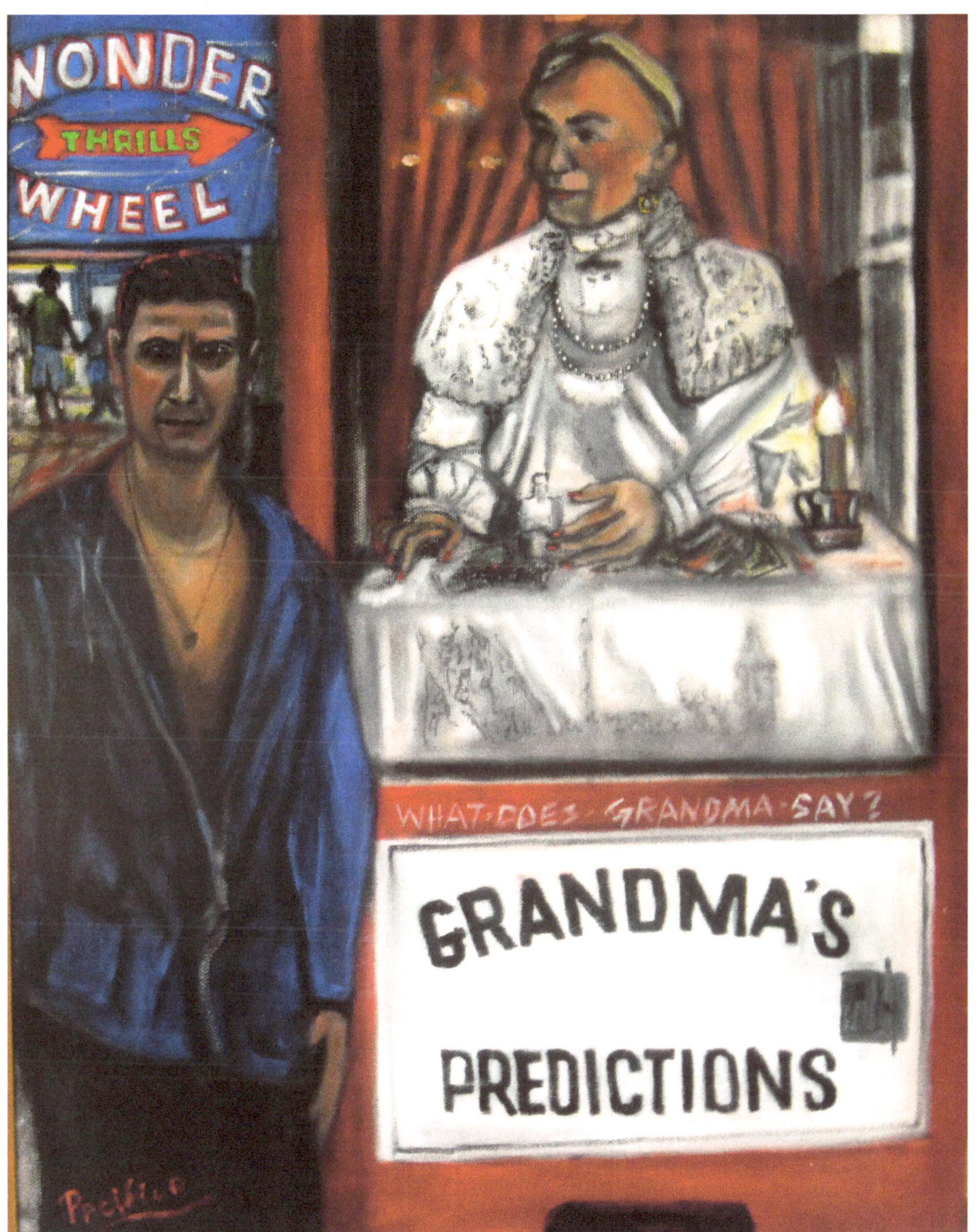
WONDER
THRILLS
WHEEL
WHAT DOES GRANDMA SAY?
GRANDMA'S
PREDICTIONS

HOT DOGS

I created this painting because I love hot dogs. It's my interpretation of how Brooklyn looked in the 1940s and early 1950s, with the trolley cars, the movie theaters, and the kids in knickers standing on a corner. I wore them too; they were fun.

I discovered the hot dog man and his cart when I started working in New York City. Back then, most of the hot dog men were Greek. I loved talking to them. They mostly sold Sabrett hot dogs. These men worked all spring, summer, and fall. If they made enough money, they spent winters back home in Greece, where it was warm. Invariably, though, a few stayed behind—so maybe they didn't make enough.

As a hot dog lover, my favorite source was Nathan's in Coney Island. My mother would give me a quarter so I could go to Coney Island, play on the beach, get two hot dogs and a root beer at Nathan's and take the trolley back home, all for 25 cents. Everything cost a nickel in those days.

I even opened a hot dog store in Greenfield, Massachusetts. I called it the Flying Dog. I sold all types of hot dogs. My favorite dog still is the New York Dog. It is a steamed hot dog on a New York–style roll, topped with sauerkraut and spicy deli mustard. I add a few chili flakes. Umm—so good.

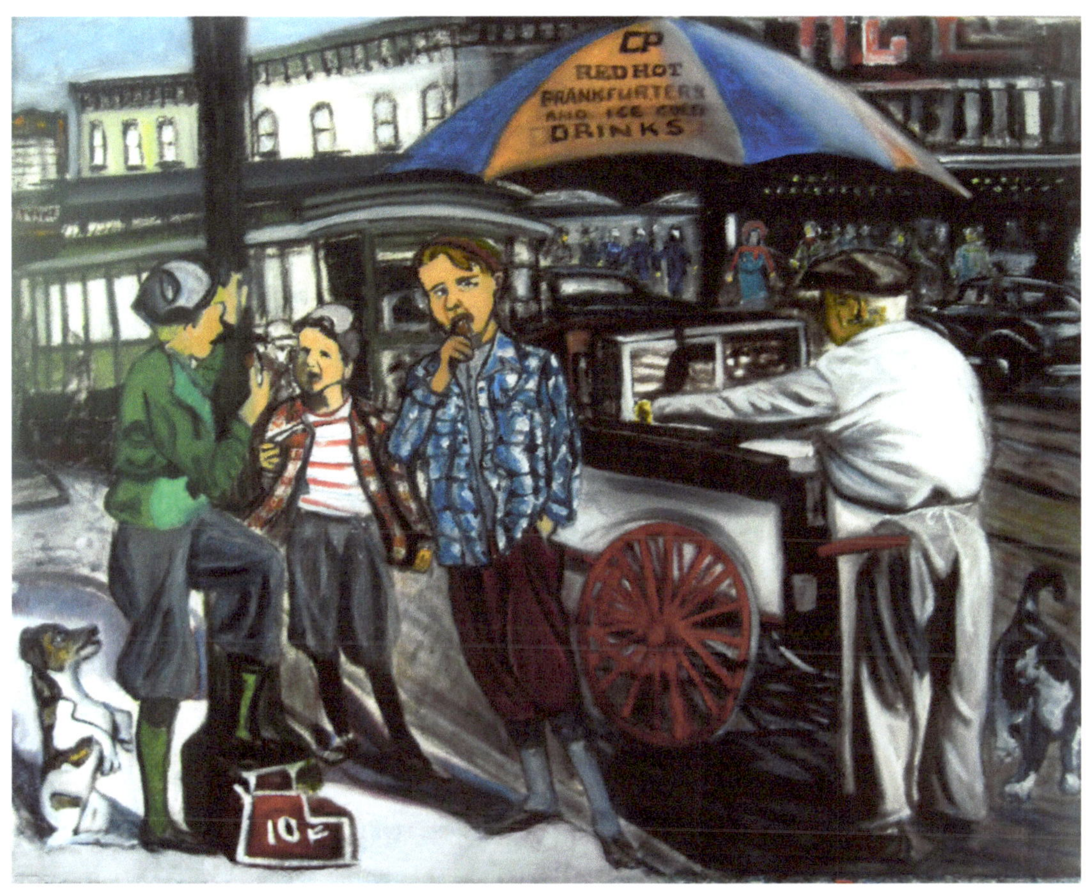
CP
RED HOT
FRANKFURTERS
DRINKS
10¢

RUFFIAN

When I first got my Nikon F camera, I took it with me everywhere. One day, I photographed my cousin Philip up against a brick wall in my parents' garden. He was about 7 or 8 years old at the time.

My Aunt Lola liked the photograph I had taken. She kept saying, "He has Grandpa's eyes." They are very large and deep. Everyone else thought that he looked like a ruffian, or gangster. I always liked Philip. In fact, he's my godchild. He was the only one strong enough to take my name, Pacifico, for his middle name at his Confirmation.

Philip is in his 50s now. These days, he lives in Boca Raton, Florida. He now looks like a "big ruffian."

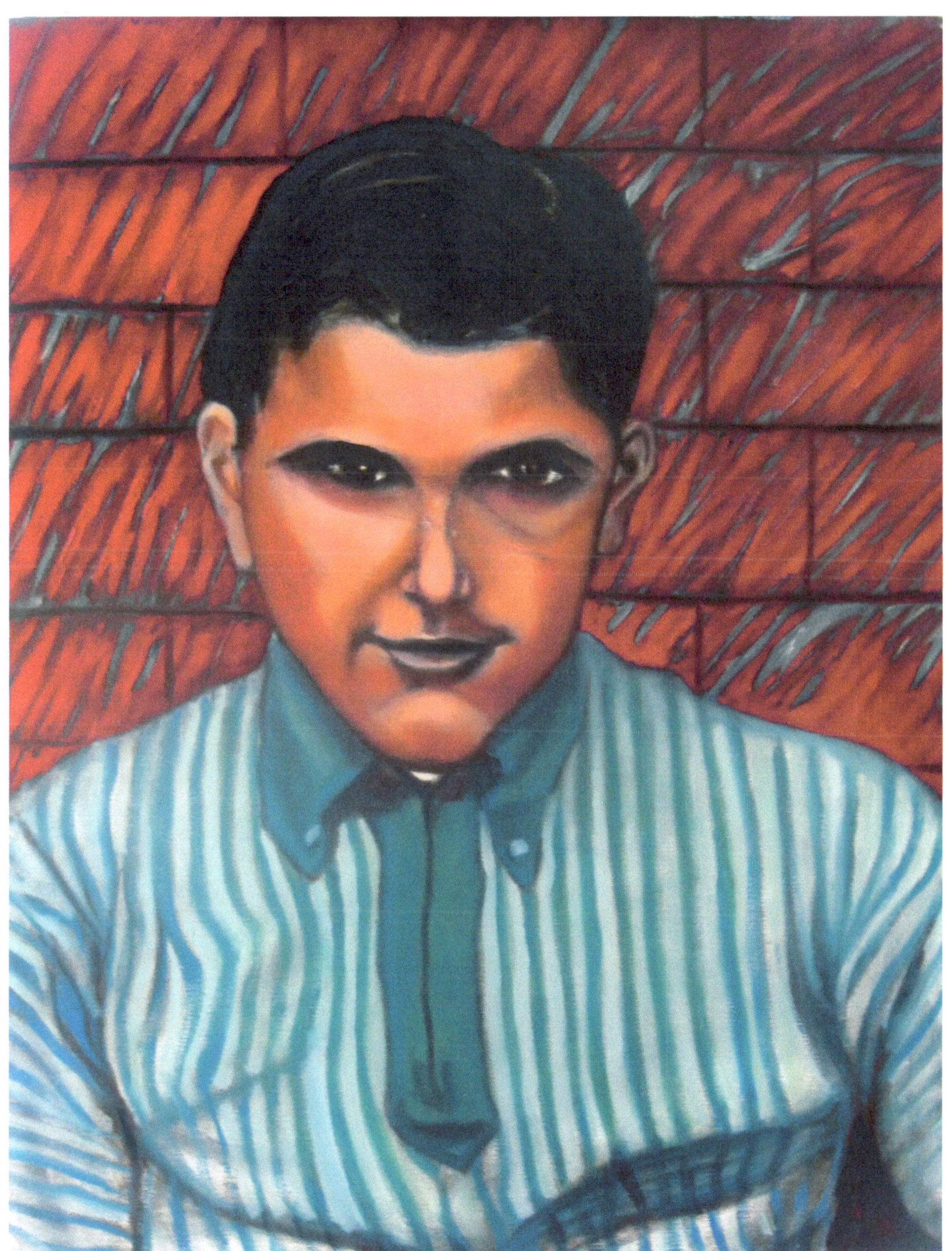

MY BEST FRIEND JIMMY & HIS WIFE LORRAINE

I have been friends with Jimmy and his wife, Lorraine, for over 55 years. I met Jimmy when I was working at the *New York Journal-American*. He and I went to Pratt Institute together and we both enjoyed painting. He replaced me as a runner from the art department to the engraving room when I was promoted to a photo retoucher

He and Lorraine were childhood sweethearts. I was best man when they were married and he was best man for me when I got married. We both enjoyed photography. He had a Nikon camera and so did I. We would go to Manhattan and photograph Times Square a lot. I painted this portrait of him as a birthday present.

They have three children and his daughter Kathleen is my godchild. We will be friends for life.

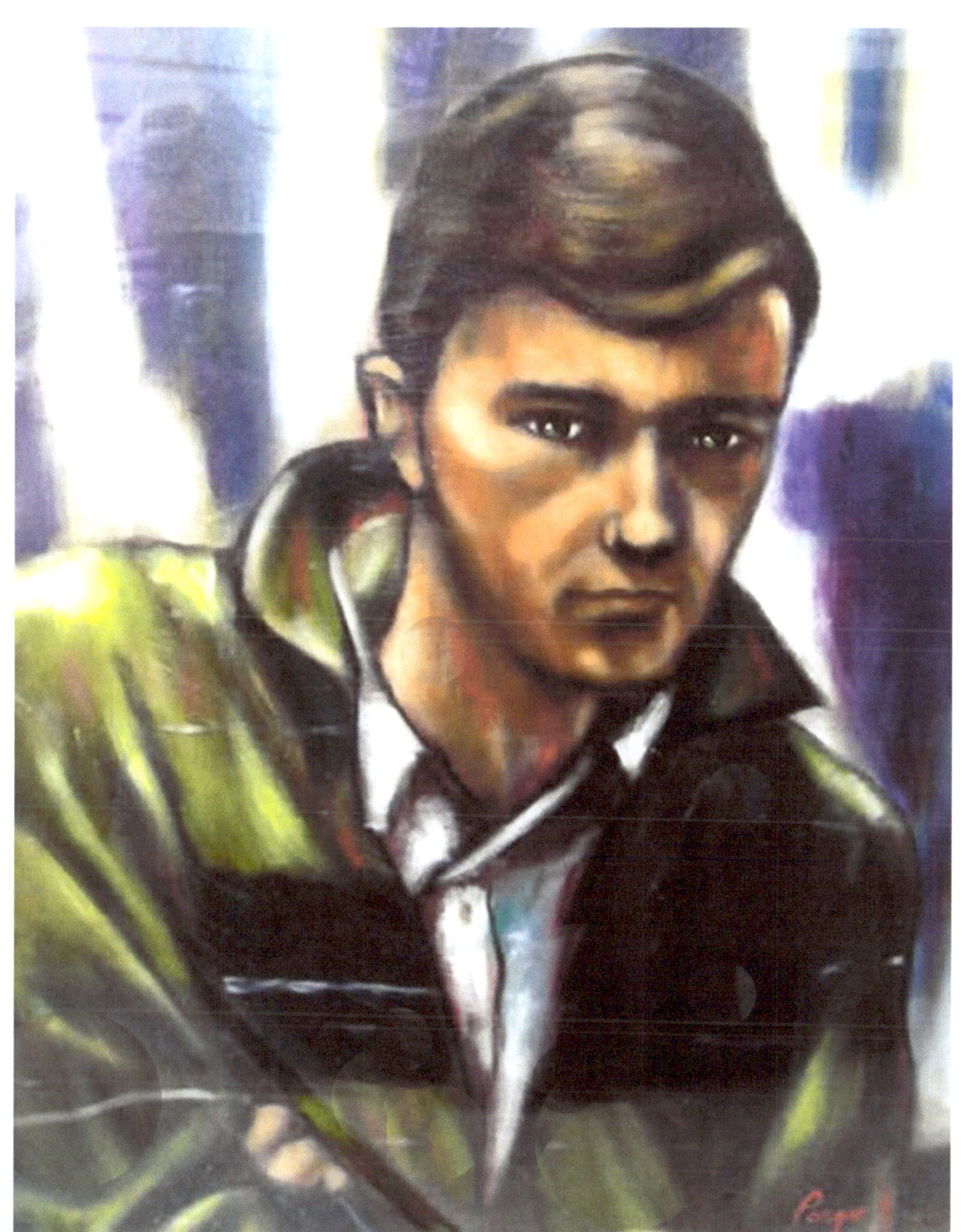

MEET MY COUSIN RICO

This is my cousin Rico from Naples. He is a relative on my father's side of the family. I photographed him while he was visiting us here in America. He was actually on his way back home to Naples with his parents when I took the photo some 35 years ago.

I found a photo of the Italian steps in a magazine and, for this painting, I put Rico in front of them. Behind him, I placed the painting by John Singer Sargent, one of my favorite artists. To fill in the gap to Rico's right, I painted in my friends Keith and Dean's dog, Curlie. I called it all "America Meet Rico."

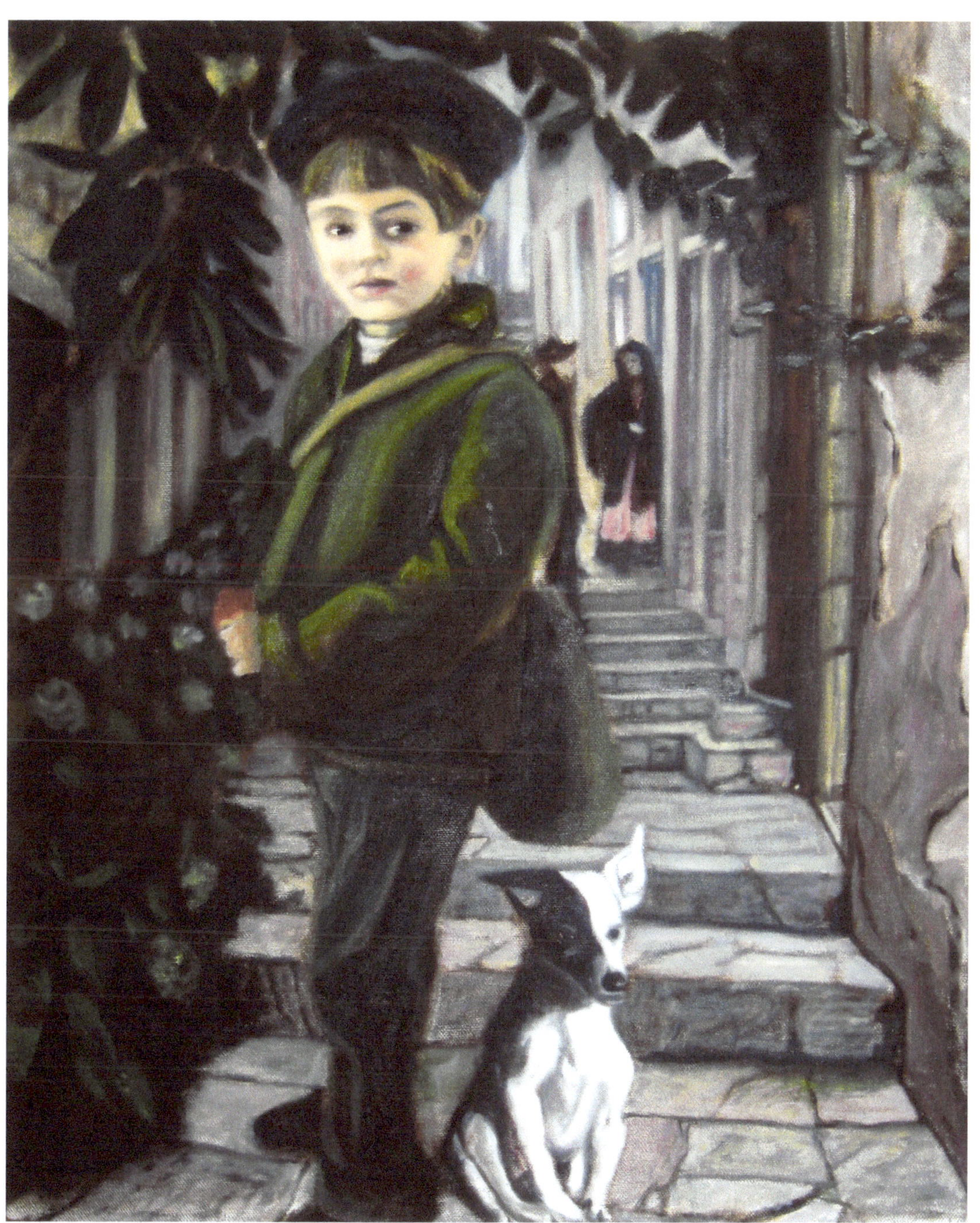

COUSIN HELENE

This is my second cousin Helene from Boca Raton, Florida. Recently, she came to our home in Massachusetts to visit with my cousin Susan, her mother, for about a week. She was with a girlfriend from New York.

While she was visiting, I told Helene that I wanted to paint a portrait of her to add to *My Italian Story.* I asked her to wear something that she liked, so she chose a scarf. I liked the one that she picked out. We had a fun visit. I hope she likes her painting.

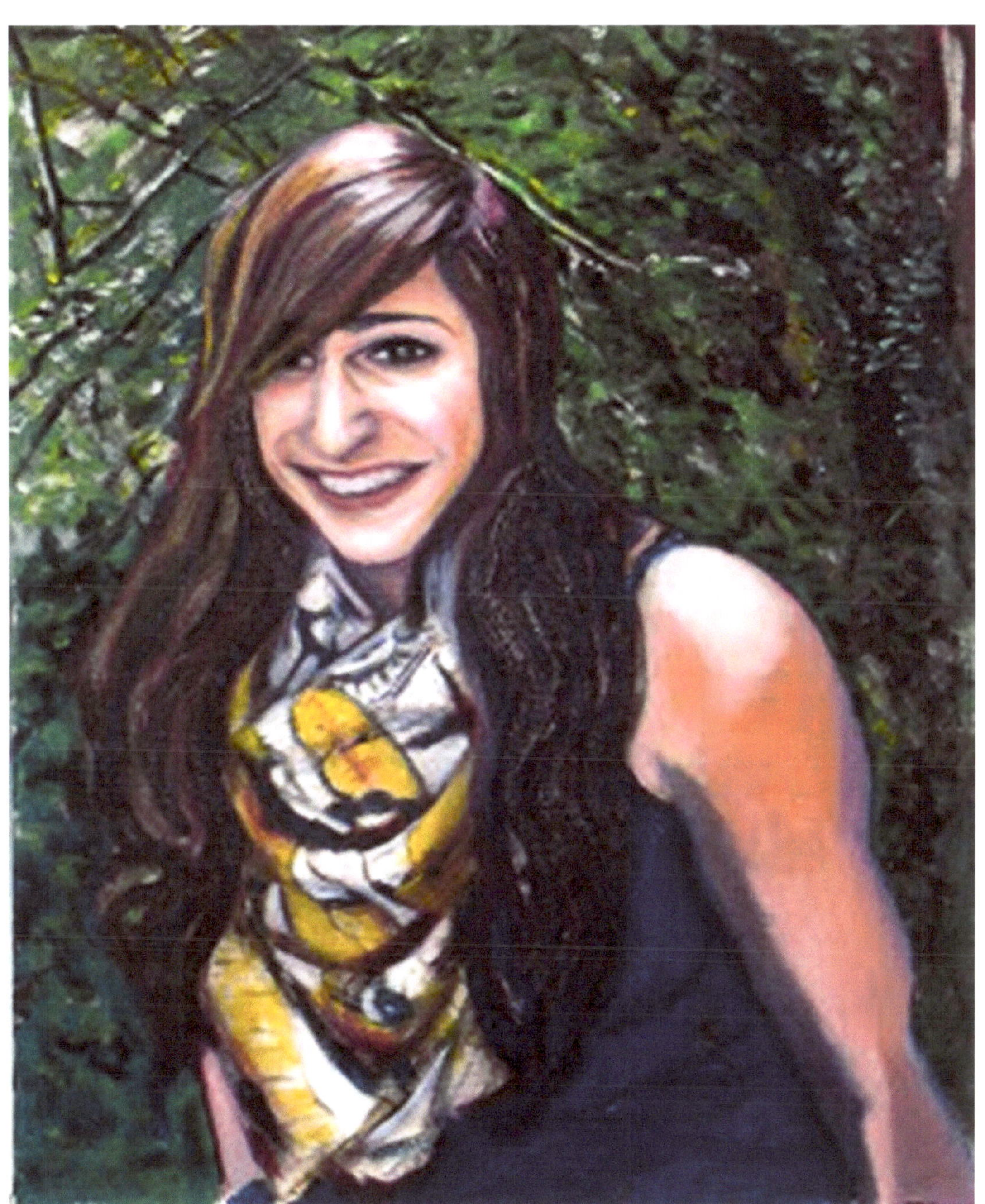

NATHAN'S HARDWARE STORE

After I was discharged from the Army, I returned to work at the *New York Journal-American*. newspaper, which was located on the lower south side of Manhattan between the Brooklyn and Manhattan Bridges.

My friend Jimmy, who worked with me there, and I would like to go scouting with our new cameras to take pictures at lunch time. We would check out the neighborhood looking for interesting subjects to photograph. This one particular time we came upon Nathans Hardware Store. It was the craziest place we ever saw. Everything was all over the place. What a great subject we thought. Then the unexpected happened. Nathan himself appeared in the doorway of the store. I have to take his picture I thought.

"Sir can I take your picture" I asked. He didn't say anything. Not a yes, not a no. He just stood there, kind of smiling not saying anything. I snapped the shutter... then I snapped it again and again. It was a great composition of Nathan standing in front of his hardware store.

I saved that shot for years. Last year I looked all over for it. Finally I found it. I have to paint it I thought. So, here it is—Nathans Hardware Store.... I added a few extras like... well, see for yourself.

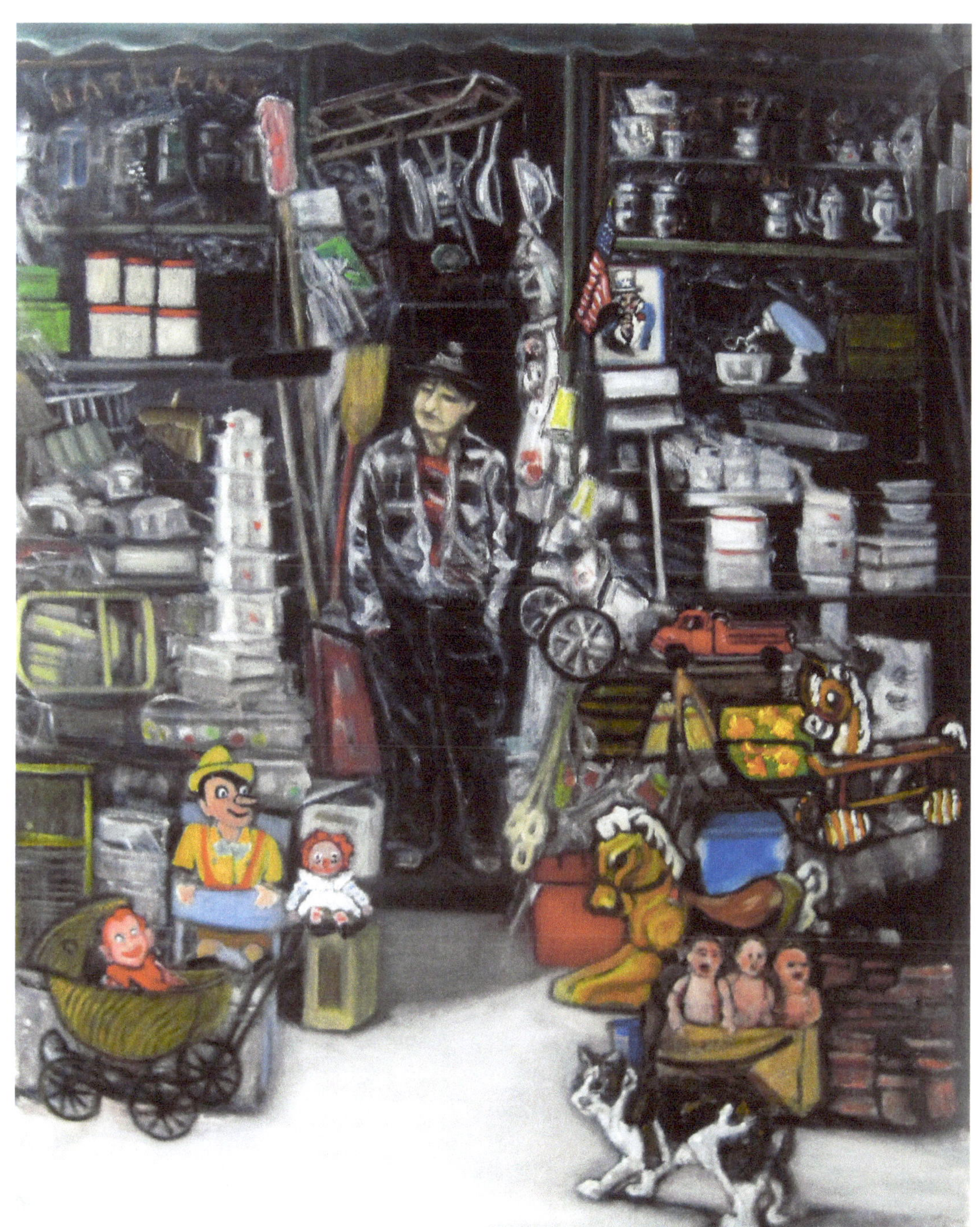

MOMMY, THESE ARE FOR YOU

I created this painting when I was 15 years old.

Every Mothers Day I would go to a local florist in our neighborhood in Brooklyn to buy the biggest bouquet of flowers I could afford to give to my mother. She would smile and give me a kiss on the my cheek. But she didn't really like flowers. I found out that they reminded her of my grandfather's funeral. Flowers to her meant death. To me they always meant joy, life and beauty.

One day I was browsing through a photography magazine and I saw this picture of a young black boy. I liked the picture and decided to paint it. I liked it because in the summer when I would go to the beach I would burn and my skin would turn very dark, so the boy reminded me of myself. I added the chair and bachelor button flowers. Even still today, it remains my favorite painting.

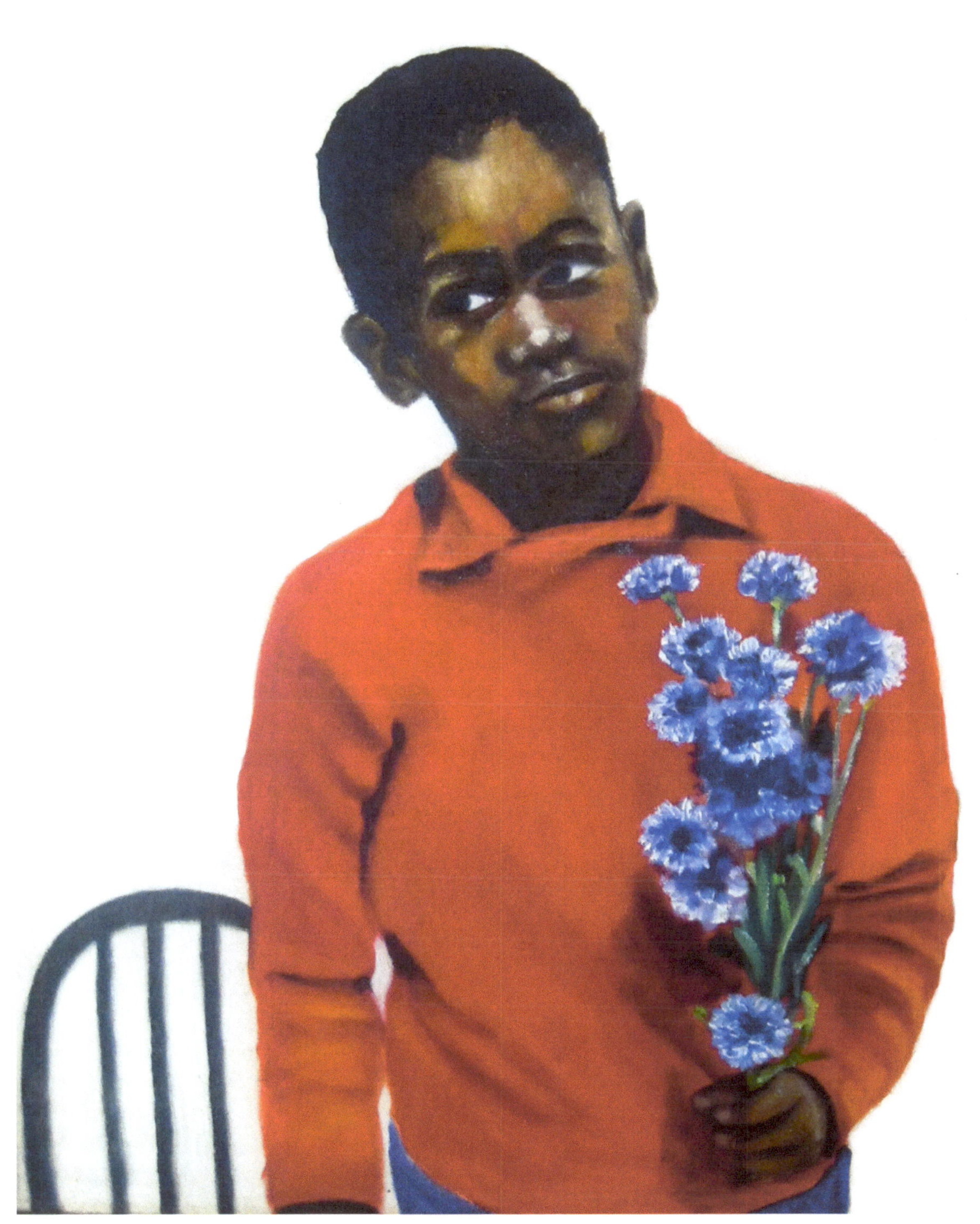

"GIVE ME SOMETHING TO REMEMBER YOU BY"

I began *My Italian Story* with the painting entitled "Daddy's Little Girl" I told you how that photo on my grandmother's mantle became the impetus for this book.

Ever since I began this book, I kept thinking about how I would end my story. I searched for the perfect painting as way to express how I feel about my family. Then I came across this painting of my Aunt Helen that I had forgotten to include. When I saw it, I realized that I had found the perfect ending. I call this painting "Give me something to remember you by." It's a painting of my Aunt Helen in my parents garden surrounded by roses. She was dressed for a wedding that we were going to.

What I would like everyone to take away from my story is my Aunt Helen's kindness. She was a warm, friendly woman, generous and considerate to all. She had a wonderful smile, one that she gave me to always remember her by.

Pacifico Palumbo
Colrain, MA
Spring 2019

Finito ~

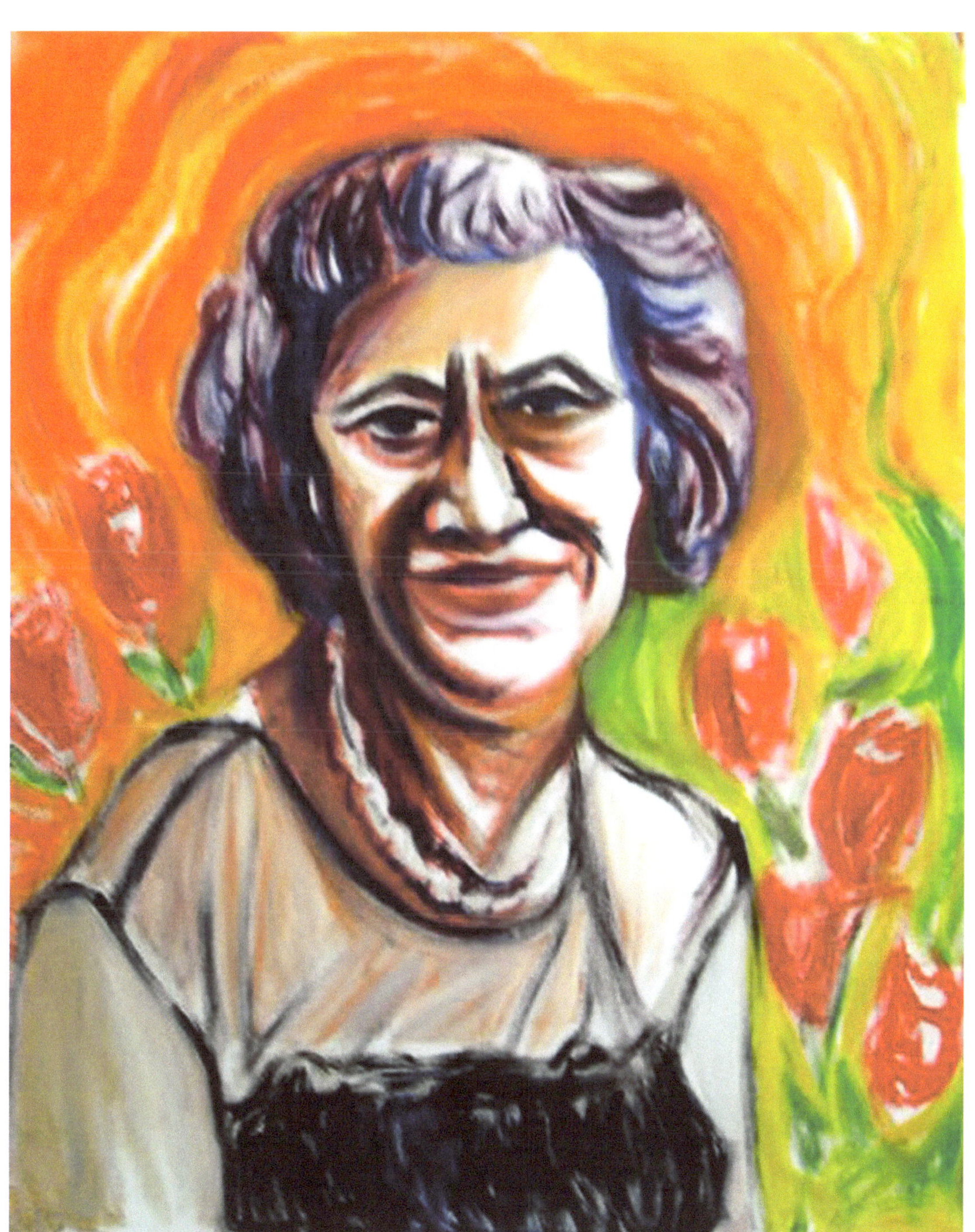

COLOPHON

The text and headings for *My Italian Story* were composed using ITC Benguiat, a font that combines graceful elegance with clear legibility. It was created by Edward Benguiat, a former jazz drummer who became a legendary font designer. Among his many designs, surely this, his namesake, is the most admired and is very well-suited to this most artful family memoir.

Maureen Moore
Booksmyth Press

www.ingramcontent.com/pod-product-compliance
Lightning Source LLC
LaVergne TN
LVHW070214110826
845147LV00003B/572

* 9 7 8 1 7 3 2 7 8 4 3 2 1 *